THE

Guys and Dolls

BOOK

The 1996 National Theatre production:
  Overleaf: Imelda Staunton as Adelaide and Henry Goodman as Nathan
  Above: The opening sequence with (left to right) Clarke Peters,
  Katy Secombe and Joanna Riding

THE

Guys and Dolls

BOOK

Original material

MATT WOLF

with contributions from

MARTY BELL
CARYL BRAHMS
RUSSELL DAVIES
STANLEY GREEN
LIFE MAGAZINE
TOM MILNE
DAMON RUNYON
NED SHERRIN
and
KENNETH TYNAN

with National Theatre photos by
JOHN HAYNES

Royal
National
Theatre

C O N T E N T S

Clive Rowe and Wayne Cater in the
1996 National Theatre Production

Damon Runyon

Alfred Damon Runyon was born in 1880 in Colorado, to Alfred Lee Runyan, a newspaper man, and Libbie J. Damon. After his mother's early death, he lived a rebellious, independent childhood, and at fifteen channeled his energies into writing for the Pueblo, Colorado, *Evening Press*. After serving in the Philippines during the Spanish-American War, Runyon returned to Colorado and wrote for several different newspapers. Besides gaining valuable writing experience, Runyon gathered a host of interesting acquaintances whom he later transformed into such characters as Nathan Detroit and Nicely-Nicely Johnson. Runyon eventually found his way to New York in 1910, where he was hired by William Randolph Hearst to write for his newspaper, the *New York American*. He quickly gained a following through his unconventional and highly entertaining rendering of the baseball world on the sports pages. Hearst soon learned to exploit his popular new commodity, and Runyon's reporting expanded to cover a variety of events until in 1926-27, with his coverage of the famous Hall-Mills and Snyder-Gray murder trials, Runyon was considered by some to be the best newspaper reporter in the United States. Runyon's success as a fiction writer began in 1929 with his Broadway stories, which he sold to such well known magazines as *Colliers, Cosmopolitan, Saturday Evening Post* and *Liberty*. In these stories, Runyon exhibited his knowledge of and affection for the strange and exciting world of Broadway, a world which he loved and inhabited for the greater portion of his life. Dream Street Rose, Louie the Lug, Harry the Horse, Little Miss Marker, Big Butch and Sky Masterson are only a few of the characters who populate Runyon's tales of the Broadway night-life and underworld. Many of his short stories, and a play which he co-wrote with Howard Lindsay called *A Slight Case of Murder*, later appeared in Hollywood film versions, some of which were produced by Runyon himself. Remaining active and productive until ill health prevented it, Damon Runyon died quietly on December 10, 1946 after a painful and difficult fight against cancer. In response to Runyon's request, his body was cremated and his ashes were scattered along his beloved Broadway.

THE IDYLL OF
MISS SARAH BROWN

Damon Runyon

O f all the high players this country ever sees, there is no doubt that the guy they call The Sky is the highest. In fact, the reason he is called The Sky is because he goes so high when it comes to betting on any proposition whatever. He will bet all he has, and nobody can bet any more than this.

His right name is Obadiah Masterson, and he is originally out of a little town in Southern Colorado where he learns to shoot craps, and play cards, and one thing and another, and where his old man is a very well-known citizen, and something of a sport himself. In fact, The Sky tells me that when he finally cleans up all the loose scratch around his home town and decides he needs more room, his old man has a little private talk with him and says to him like this:

'Son,' the old guy says, 'you are now going out into the wide, wide world to make your own way, and it is a very good thing to do, as there are no more opportunities for you in this burg. I am only sorry,' he says, 'that I am not able to bank-roll you to a very large start, but,' he says, 'not having any potatoes to give you, I am now going to stake you to some very valuable advice, which I personally collect in my years of experience around and about, and I hope and trust you will always bear this advice in mind.

Shooting Craps

Equipment

1. Two dice, numbered so that the spots on opposite sides of each die add up to seven.
2. A backboard or wall against which the dice are thrown.

The Players

1. Any number can play.
2. One player, by common consent of the rest of the players, is chosen to make the first throw of the dice. The player throwing the dice is called the *shooter*.
3. The dice pass around the circle of players to the left.

The Play

1. The shooter throws the dice and the two numbers facing upward when the dice come to rest, added together, are the deciding numbers.
2. If on the first roll, called the *come-out*, the shooter throws:
   a *natural* (7 or 11), it is a winning decision, or *pass*;
   a *crap* (2, 3, or 12), it is a losing decision, or *missout*;
   4, 5, 6, 8, 9, or 10, that number becomes the shooter's *point*, and the shooter continues throwing until either he/she:
   makes the point by throwing the same number again, thereby making a winning decision or pass,
   or, throws a 7, thereby making a losing decision or missout.
3. If the player does not make the point, the dice are passed to the next player on the left, who becomes the new shooter.
4. Any player may refuse to shoot in his/her turn and pass the dice along to the next player. If the shooter chooses, he/she may pass the dice to the next player on the completion of any deciding throw, without waiting to missout on a point throw.

Betting

1. *Right bet.* A bet that the dice will pass either by making a natural on the come-out roll or by throwing a point and then repeating it before throwing a 7.
2. *Wrong bet.* A bet that the dice will missout either by making a crap on the come-out or by failing to repeat a point.
3. *Center bet.* Before the come-out roll, the shooter may wager that he/she will pass by placing a wager in the center of the playing area. Players betting that the shooter will missout are said to be *fading* the shooter. They may cover all or a part of the wager the shooter has placed in the center. If only a part of the shooter's center bet is covered by the other players, he/she may call off the bet by saying "no bet."
4. *Side bet.* Any bet that is not a center bet is placed at the side of the playing area and is known as a *side bet*. All the remaining bets in this list are side bets.
5. *Flat bet.* A side bet made before the come-out roll that the dice pass or don't pass. The same as a center bet except that the shooter is not being faded and the bet is placed on the side of the playing area.
6. *Point bet.* A bet that the shooter will or will not make his/her point. This bet is made *after* the shooter has thrown a point on the come-out roll. A bet made by a right bettor that the shooter makes his point is a *right point bet*. A bet by a wrong bettor that the shooter misses his point is a *wrong point bet*. The right bettor *takes the odds* on that point; the wrong bettor *lays the odds*.
7. *Come bet.* A bet that the dice will pass, or win; the next roll to be considered a come-out roll. This bet is made (on any of the rolls) after the shooter has thrown a point.
8. *Don't come bet.* A bet that the dice don't pass, or lose; the next roll to be considered a come-out roll.
9. *Other side bets.* Several other side bets may be made, usually that a certain number will be thrown in a certain way (**the hard way,** for example, in which an even number is thrown with the same number of spots showing on each die, double-four, double-six, etc.), or that a certain number or series of numbers will appear or not appear before another number during a succession of throws.
10. All bets must be made before the dice are thrown and cannot be made while they are rolling.

A wise gamester ought to take the dice
Even as they fall, and pay down quietly,
Rather than grumble at his luck.
— *Sophocles*

'Son,' the old guy says, 'no matter how far you travel, or how smart you get, always remember this: Some day, somewhere,' he says, 'a guy is going to come to you and show you a nice brand-new deck of cards on which the seal is never broken, and this guy is going to offer to bet you that the jack of spades will jump out of this deck and squirt cider in your ear. But, son,' the old guy says, 'do not bet him, for as sure as you do you are going to get an ear full of cider.'

Well, The Sky remembers what his old man says, and he is always very cautious about betting on such propositions as the jack of spades jumping out of a sealed deck of cards and squirting cider in his ear, and so he makes few mistakes as he goes along. In fact, the only real mistake The Sky makes is when he hits St. Louis after leaving his old home town, and loses all his potatoes betting a guy St. Louis is the biggest town in the world.

Now of course this is before The Sky ever sees any bigger towns, and he is never much of a hand for reading up on matters such as this. In fact, the only reading The Sky ever does as he goes along through life is in these Gideon Bibles such as he finds in the hotel rooms where he lives, for The Sky never lives anywhere else but in hotel rooms for years.

He tells me that he reads many items of great interest in these Gideon Bibles, and furthermore The Sky says that several times these Gideon Bibles keep him from getting out of line, such as the time he finds himself pretty much frozen-in over in Cincinnati, what with owing everybody in town except maybe the mayor from playing games of chance of one kind and another.

Well, The Sky says he sees no way of meeting these obligations and he is figuring the only thing he can do is to take a run-out powder, when he happens to read in one of these Gideon Bibles where it says like this:

'Better is it,' the Gideon Bible says, 'that thou shouldest not vow, than that thou shouldest vow and not pay.'

Well, The Sky says he can see that there is no doubt whatever but that

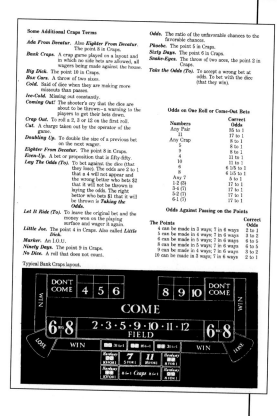

this means a guy shall not welsh, so he remains in Cincinnati until he manages to wiggle himself out of the situation, and from that day to this, The Sky never thinks of welshing.

He is maybe thirty years old, and is a tall guy with a round kisser, and big blue eyes, and he always looks as innocent as a little baby. But The Sky is by no means as innocent as he looks. In fact, The Sky is smarter than three Philadelphia lawyers, which makes him very smart, indeed, and he is well established as a high player in New Orleans, and Chicago, and Los Angeles, and wherever else there is any action in the way of card-playing, or crap-shooting, or horse-racing, or betting on the baseball games, for The Sky is always moving around the country following the action.

But while The Sky will bet on anything whatever, he is more of a short-card player and a crap-shooter than anything else, and furthermore he is a great hand for propositions, such as are always coming up among citizens who follow games of chance for a living. Many citizens prefer betting on propositions to anything you can think of, because they figure a proposition gives them a chance to out-smart somebody, and in fact I know citizens who will sit up all night making up propositions to offer other citizens the next day.

A proposition may be only a problem in cards, such as what is the price against a guy getting aces back-to-back, or how often a pair of deuces will win a hand in stud, and then again it may be some very daffy proposition, indeed, although the daffier any proposition seems to be, the more citizens like it. And no one ever sees The Sky when he does not have some proposition of his own.

The first time he ever shows up around this town, he goes to a baseball game at the Polo Grounds with several prominent citizens, and while he is at the ball game, he buys himself a sack of Harry Stevens' peanuts, which he dumps in a side pocket of his coat. He is eating these peanuts all through the game, and after the game is over and he is walking across the field with the citizens, he says to them like this:

'What price,' The Sky says, 'I cannot throw a peanut from second base to the home plate?'

Well, everybody knows that a peanut is too light for anybody to throw it this far, so Big Nig, the crap shooter, who always likes to have a little the best of it running for him, speaks as follows:

'You can have 3 to 1 from me, stranger,' Big Nig says.

'Two C's against six,' The Sky says, and then he stands on second base, and takes a peanut out of his pocket, and not only whips it to the home plate, but on into the lap of a fat guy who is still sitting in the grand stand putting the zing on Bill Terry for not taking Walker out of the box when Walker is getting a pasting from the other club.

Well, naturally, this is a most astonishing throw, indeed, but afterwards it comes out that The Sky throws a peanut loaded with lead, and of course it is not one of Harry Stevens' peanuts, either, as Harry is not selling peanuts full of lead at a dime a bag, with the price of lead what it is.

It is only a few nights after this that the Sky states another most unusual proposition to a group of citizens sitting in Mindy's restaurant when he offers to bet a C note that he can go down into Mindy's cellar and catch a live rat with his bare hands and everybody is greatly astonished when Mindy himself steps up and takes the bet, for ordinarily Mindy will not bet you a nickel he is alive.

But it seems that Mindy knows that The Sky plants a tame rat in the cellar, and this rat knows The Sky and loves him dearly, and will let him catch it any time he wishes, and it also seems that Mindy knows that one of his dish washers happens upon this rat, and not knowing it is tame, knocks it flatter than a pancake. So when The Sky goes down into the cellar and starts trying to catch a rat with his bare hands he is greatly surprised how inhospitable the rat turns out to be, because it is one of Mindy's personal rats, and Mindy is around afterwards saying he will lay plenty of 7 to 5 against even Strangler Lewis being able to catch one of his rats with his bare hands, or with boxing gloves on.

I am only telling you all this to show you what a smart guy The Sky is, and I am only sorry I do not have time to tell you about many other very remarkable propositions that he thinks up outside of his regular business.

It is well-known to one and all that he is very honest in every respect, and that he hates and despises cheaters at cards, or dice, and furthermore The Sky never wishes to play with any the best of it himself, or anyway not much. He will never take the inside of any situation, as many gamblers love to do, such as owning a gambling house, and having the percentage run for him instead of against him, for always The Sky is strictly a player, because he says he will never care to settle down in one spot long enough to become the owner of anything.

In fact, in all the years The Sky is drifting around the country, nobody ever knows him to own anything except maybe a bank roll, and when he comes to Broadway the last time, which is the time I am now speaking of, he has a hundred G's in cash money, and an extra suit of clothes, and this is all he has in the world. He never owns such a thing as a house, or an automobile, or a piece of jewellery. He never owns a watch, because The Sky says time means nothing to him.

Of course some guys will figure a hundred G's comes under the head of owning something, but as far as The Sky is concerned, money is nothing but just something for him to play with and the dollars may as well be doughnuts as far as value goes with him. The only time The Sky ever thinks of money as money is when he is broke, and the only way he can tell he is broke is when he reaches into his pocket and finds nothing there but his fingers.

Then it is necessary for The Sky to go and dig up some fresh scratch somewhere, and when it comes to digging up scratch, The Sky is practically supernatural. He can get more potatoes on the strength of a telegram to some place or other than John D. Rockefeller can get on collateral, for everybody knows The Sky's word is as good as wheat in the bin.

Now one Sunday evening The Sky is walking along Broadway, and at the corner of Forty-ninth Street he comes upon a little bunch of mission workers who are holding a religious meeting, such as mission workers love to do of a Sunday evening, the idea being that they may round up a few sinners here and there, although personally I always claim the mission workers come out too early to catch any sinners on this part of Broadway. At such an hour the sinners are still in bed resting up from their sinning of the night before, so they will be in good shape for more sinning a little later on.

There are only four of these mission workers, and two of them are old guys, and one is an old doll, while the other is a young doll who is tootling on a cornet. And after a couple of ganders at this young doll, The Sky is a goner, for this is one of the most beautiful young dolls anybody ever sees on Broadway, and especially as a mission worker. Her name is Miss Sarah Brown.

She is tall, and thin, and has a first-class shape, and her hair is a light brown, going on blonde, and her eyes are like I do not know what, except that they are one-hundred-per-cent eyes in every respect. Furthermore, she is not a bad cornet player, if you like cornet players, although at this spot on Broadway she has to play against a scat band in a chop-suey joint near by, and this is tough competition, although at that many citizens believe Miss Sarah Brown will win by a large score if only she gets a little more support from one of the old guys with her who has a big bass drum, but does not pound it hearty enough.

Well, The Sky stands there listening to Miss Sarah Brown tootling on the cornet for quite a spell, and then he hears her make a speech in which she puts the blast on sin very good, and boosts religion quite some, and says if there are any souls around that need saving the owners of the same may step forward at once. But no one steps forward, so The Sky comes over to Mindy's restaurant where many citizens are congregated, and starts telling us about Miss Sarah Brown. But of course we already know about Miss Sarah Brown, because she is so beautiful, and so good.

Furthermore, everybody feels somewhat sorry for Miss Sarah Brown, for while she is always tootling the cornet, and making speeches, and looking to save any souls that need saving, she never seems to find any souls to save, or at least her bunch of mission workers never gets any bigger. In fact, it gets smaller, as she starts out with a guy who plays a very fair sort of trombone, but this guy takes it on the lam one night with the trombone, which one and all consider a dirty trick.

Now from this time on, The Sky does not take any interest in anything but Miss Sarah Brown, and any night she is out on the corner with the other mission workers, you will see The Sky standing around looking at her, and naturally after a few weeks of this, Miss Sarah Brown must know The Sky is looking at her, or she is dumber than seems possible. And nobody ever figures Miss Sarah Brown dumb, as she is always on her toes, and seems

'Well, it seems from what Miss Sarah Brown says the soul-saving is very slow, indeed, these days.'
Paul Jones (Sky), John Normington (Arvide), Belinda Sinclair (Sarah) and Robert Ralph (Calvin) in
the re-cast 1982 National Theatre production.

plenty able to take care of herself, even on Broadway.

Sometimes after the street meeting is over, The Sky follows the mission workers to their headquarters in an old storeroom around in Forty-eighth Street where they generally hold an indoor session, and I hear The Sky drops many a large coarse note in the collection box while looking at Miss Sarah Brown, and there is no doubt these notes come in handy around the mission, as I hear business is by no means good there.

It is called the Save-a-Soul Mission, and it is run mainly by Miss Sarah Brown's grandfather, an old guy with whiskers, by the name of Arvide Abernathy, but Miss Sarah Brown seems to do most of the work, including tootling the cornet, and visiting the poor people around and about, and all this and that, and many citizens claim it is a great shame that such a beautiful doll is wasting her time being good.

How The Sky ever becomes acquainted with Miss Sarah Brown is a very great mystery, but the next thing anybody knows, he is saying hello to her, and she is smiling at him out of her one-hundred-per-cent eyes, and one evening when I happen to be with The Sky we run into her walking along Forty-ninth Street, and The Sky hauls off and stops her, and says it is a nice evening, which it is, at that. Then The Sky says to Miss Sarah Brown like this:

'Well,' The Sky says, 'how is the mission dodge going these days? Are you saving any souls?' he says.

Well, it seems from what Miss Sarah Brown says the soul-saving is very slow, indeed, these days.

'In fact,' Miss Sarah Brown says, 'I worry greatly about how few souls we seem to save. Sometimes I wonder if we are lacking in grace.'

She goes on up the street, and The Sky stands looking after her, and he says to me like this:

'I wish I can think of some way to help this little doll,' he says, 'especially,' he says, 'in saving a few souls to build up her mob at the mission. I must speak to her again, and see if I can figure something out.'

But The Sky does not get to speak to Miss Sarah Brown again, because somebody weighs in the sacks on him by telling her he is nothing but a professional gambler, and that he is a very undesirable character, and that his only interest in hanging around the mission is because she is a good-looking doll. So all of a sudden Miss Sarah Brown plays a plenty of chill for The Sky. Furthermore, she sends him word that she does not care to accept any more of his potatoes in the collection box, because his potatoes are nothing but ill-gotten gains.

Well, naturally, this hurts The Sky's feeling no little, so he quits standing around looking at Miss Sarah Brown, and going to the mission, and takes to mingling with the citizens in Mindy's, and showing some interest in the affairs of the community, especially the crap games.

Of course the crap games that are going on at this time are nothing much, because practically everybody in the world is broke, but there is a head-and-head game run by Nathan Detroit over a garage in Fifty-second Street where there is occasionally some action, and who shows up at this crap game early one evening but The Sky, although it seems he shows up there more to find company than anything else.

In fact, he only stands around watching the play, and talking to the other guys who are also standing around and watching, and many of these guys are very high shots during the gold rush, although most of them are now as clean as a jaybird, and maybe cleaner. One of these guys is a guy by the name of Brandy Bottle Bates, who is known from coast to coast as a high player when he has anything to play with, and who is called Brandy Bottle Bates because it seems that years ago he is a great hand for belting a brandy bottle around.

This Brandy Bottle Bates is a big, black-looking guy, with a large beezer, and a head shaped like a pear, and he is considered a very immoral and wicked character, but he is a pretty slick gambler, and a fast man with a dollar when he is in the money.

Well, finally The Sky asks Brandy Bottle why he is not playing and Brandy laughs, and states as follows:

'Why,' he says, 'in the first place I have no potatoes, and in the second place I doubt if it will do me much good to have any potatoes the way I am going the past year. Why,' Brandy Bottle says, 'I cannot win a bet to save my soul.'

Now this crack seems to give The Sky an idea, as he stands looking at Brandy Bottle very strangely, and while he is looking, Big Nig, the crap shooter, picks up the dice and hits three times hand-running, bing, bing,

THE GUYS AND DOLLS BOOK

bing. Then Big Nig comes out on a six and Brandy Bottle Bates speaks as follows:

'You see how my luck is,' he says. 'Here is Big Nig hotter than a stove, and here I am without a bob to follow him with, especially,' Brandy says, 'when he is looking for nothing but a six. Why,' he says, 'Nig can make sixes all night when he is hot. If he does not make this six, the way he is, I will be willing to turn square and quit gambling forever.'

'Well, Brandy,' The Sky says, 'I will make you a proposition. I will lay you a G note Big Nig does not get his six. I will lay you a G note against nothing but your soul,' he says. 'I mean if Big Nig does not get his six, you are to turn square and join Miss Sarah Brown's mission for six months.'

'Bet!' Brandy Bottle Bates says right away, meaning the proposition is on, although chances are he does not quite understand the proposition. All Brandy understands is The Sky wishes to wager that Big Nig does not make his six, and Brandy bottle Bates will be willing to bet his soul a couple of times over on Big Nig making his six, and figure he is getting the best of it at that, as Brandy has great confidence in Nig.

Well, sure enough, Big Nig makes the six, so The Sky weeds Brandy Bottle Bates a G note, although everybody around is saying The Sky makes a terrible over-lay of the natural price in giving Brandy Bottle a G against his soul. Furthermore, everybody around figures the chances are The Sky only wishes to give Brandy an opportunity to get in action, and nobody figures The Sky is on the level about trying to win Brandy Bates' soul, especially as The Sky odes not seem to wish to go any further after paying the bet.

He only stands there looking on and seeming somewhat depressed as Brandy Bottle goes into action on his own account with the G note, fading other guys around the table with cash money. But Brandy Bottle Bates seems to figure what is in The Sky's mind pretty well, because Brandy Bottle is a crafty old guy.

It finally comes to his turn to handle the dice, and he hits a couple of times, and then he comes out on a four, and anybody will tell you that a four is a very tough point to make, even with a lead pencil. Then Brandy Bottle turns to The Sky and speaks to him as follows:

'Well, Sky,' he says, 'I will take the odds off you on this one. I know you do not want my dough,' he says. 'I know you only want my soul for

Miss Sarah Brown, and,' he says, 'without wishing to be fresh about it, I know why you want it for her. I am young once myself,' Brandy Bottle says. 'And you know if I lose to you, I will be over there in Forty-eighth Street in an hour pounding on the door, for Brandy always settles.

'But, Sky,' he says, 'now I am in the money, and my price goes up. Will you lay me ten G's against my soul I do not make this four?'

'Bet!' The Sky says, and right away Brandy Bottle hits with a four.

Well, when word goes around that The Sky is up at Nathan Detroit's crap game trying to win Brandy Bottle Bates' soul for Miss Sarah Brown, the excitement is practically intense. Somebody telephones Mindy's where a large number of citizens are sitting around arguing about this and that, and telling one another how much they will bet in support of their arguments, if only they have something to bet, and Mindy himself is almost killed in the rush for the door.

One of the first guys out of Mindy's and up to the crap game is Regret, the horse player, and as he comes in Brandy Bottle is looking for a nine, and The Sky is laying him twelve G's against his soul that he does not make his nine, for it seems Brandy Bottle's soul keeps getting more and more expensive.

Well, Regret wishes to bet his soul against a G that Brandy Bottle gets his nine, and is greatly insulted when The Sky cannot figure his price any better than a double saw, but finally Regret accepts this price, and Brandy Bottle hits again.

Now many other citizens request a little action from The Sky, and if there is one thing The Sky cannot deny a citizen it is action, so he says he will lay them according to how he figures their word to join Miss Sarah Brown's mission if Brandy Bottle misses out, but about this time The Sky finds he has no more potatoes on him, being now around thirty-five G's loser, and he wishes to give markers.

But Brandy Bottle says that while ordinarily he will be pleased to extend The Sky this accommodation, he does not care to accept markers against his soul, so then The Sky has to leave the joint and go over to his hotel two or three blocks away, and get the night clerk to open his damper so The Sky can get the rest of his bank roll. In the meantime the crap game continues at Nathan Detroit's among the small operators, while the other citizens stand around and say that while they hear of many a daffy proposition in their time, this is the daffiest that ever comes to their attention, although Big Nig claims he hears of a daffier one, but cannot think what it is.

Big Nig claims that all gamblers are daffy anyway, and in fact he says if they are not daffy they will not be gamblers, and while he is arguing this matter back comes The Sky with fresh scratch, and Brandy Bottle Bates takes up where he leaves off, although Brandy says he is accepting the worst of it, as the dice have a chance to cool off.

Now the upshot of the whole business is that Brandy Bottle hits thirteen licks in a row, and the last lick he makes is on a ten, and it is for twenty G's against his soul, with about a dozen other citizens getting anywhere from one to five C's against their souls, and complaining bitterly of the price.

And as Brandy Bottle makes his ten, I happen to look at The Sky and I see him watching Brandy with a very peculiar expression on his face, and furthermore I see The Sky's right hand creeping inside his coat where I know he always packs a Betsy in a shoulder holster, so I can see something is wrong somewhere.

But before I can figure out what it is, there is quite a fuss at the door, and loud talking, and a doll's voice, and all of a sudden in bobs nobody else but Miss Sarah Brown. It is plain to be seen that she is all steamed up about something.

She marches right up to the crap table where Brandy Bottle Bates and The Sky and the other citizens are standing, and one and all are feeling sorry for Dobber, the doorman, thinking of what Nathan Detroit is bound to say to him for letting her in. The dice are still lying on the table showing Brandy Bottle Bates' last throw, which cleans The Sky and gives many citizens the first means they enjoy in several months.

Well, Miss Sarah Brown looks at The Sky, and The Sky looks at Miss Sarah Brown, and Miss Sarah Brown looks at the citizens around and about, and one and all are somewhat dumbfounded, and nobody seems to be able to think of much to say, although The Sky finally speaks up as follows:

'Good evening,' The Sky says. 'It is a nice evening,' he says. 'I am trying to win a few souls for you around here, but,' he says, 'I seem to be about half out of luck.'

'Well,' Miss Sarah Brown says, looking at The Sky most severely out of her hundred-per-cent eyes, 'you are taking too much upon yourself. I can win any souls I need myself. You better be thinking of your own soul. By the way,' she says, 'are you risking your own soul, or just the money?'

Well, of course up to this time The Sky is not risking anything but his potatoes, so he only shakes his head to Miss Sarah Brown's question, and looks somewhat disorganized.

'I know something about gambling,' Miss Sarah Brown says, 'especially about crap games. I ought to,' she says. 'It ruins my poor papa and my brother Joe. If you wish to gamble for souls, Mister Sky, gamble for your own soul.'

Now Miss Sarah Brown opens a small black leather pocketbook she is carrying in one hand, and pulls out a two-dollar bill, and it is such a two-dollar bill as seems to have seen much service in its time, and holding up this deuce, Miss Sarah Brown speaks as follows:

'I will gamble with you, Mister Sky,' she says. 'I will gamble with you,' she says, 'on the same terms you gamble with these parties here. This two dollars against your soul, Mister Sky. It is all I have, but,' she says, 'it is more than your soul is worth.'

Well, of course anybody can see that Miss Sarah Brown is doing this because she is very angry, and wishes to make The Sky look small, but right away the Sky's duke comes from inside his coat, and he picks up the dice and hands them to her and speaks as follows:

'Roll them,' The Sky says, and Miss Sarah Brown snatches the dice out of his hand and gives them a quick sling on the table in such a way that anybody can see she is not a professional crap shooter, and not even an amateur crap shooter, for all amateur crap shooters first breathe on the dice, and rattle them good, and make remarks to them, such as 'Come on, baby!'

In fact, there is some criticism of Miss Sarah Brown afterwards on account of her haste, as many citizens are eager to string with her to hit, while others are just as anxious to bet she misses, and she does not give them a chance to get down.

Well, Scranton Slim is the stick guy, and he takes a gander at the dice as they hit up against the side of the table and bounce back, and then Slim hollers, 'Winner, winner, winner,' as stick guys love to do, and what is showing on the dice as big as life, but a six and a five, which makes eleven, no matter how you figure, so The Sky's soul belongs to Miss Sarah Brown.

She turns at once and pushes through the citizens at the table without even waiting to pick up the deuce she lays down when she grabs the dice. Afterwards a most obnoxious character by the name of Red Nose Regan tries to claim the deuce as a sleeper and gets the heave-o from Nathan Detroit, who becomes very indignant about this, stating that Red Nose is trying to give his joint a wrong rap.

Naturally, The Sky follows Miss Brown, and Dobber, the doorman, tells me that as they are waiting for him to unlock the door and let them out, Miss Sarah Brown turns on The Sky and speaks to him as follows:

'You are a fool,' Miss Sarah Brown says.

Well, at this Dobber figures The Sky is bound to let one go, as this seems to be the most insulting language, but instead of letting one go, The Sky only smiles at Miss Sarah Brown and says to her like this:

'Why,' The Sky says, 'Paul says "If any man among you seemeth to be wise in the world, let him become a fool, that he may be wise." I love you, Miss Sarah Brown,' The Sky says.

Well, now, Dobber has a pretty fair sort of memory, and he says that Miss Sarah Brown tells The Sky that since he seems to know so much about the Bible, maybe he remembers the second verse of the Song of Solomon, but the chances are Dobber muffs the number of the verse, because I look the matter up in one of these Gideon Bibles, and the verse seems a little too much for Miss Sarah Brown, although of course you never can tell.

Anyway, this is about all there is to the story, except that Brandy Bottle Bates slides out during the confusion so quietly even Dobber scarcely remembers letting him out, and he takes most of The Sky's potatoes with him, but he soon gets batted in against the faro bank out in Chicago, and the last anybody hears of him he gets religion all over again, and is preaching out in San Jose, so The Sky always claims he beats Brandy for his soul, at that.

I see The Sky the other night at Forty-ninth Street and Broadway, and he is with quite a raft of mission workers, including Mrs. Sky, for it seems that the soul-saving business picks up wonderfully, and The Sky is giving a big bass drum such a first-class whacking that the scat band in the chop-suey joint can scarcely be heard. Furthermore, The Sky is hollering between whacks, and I never see a guy look happier, especially when Mrs. Sky smiles at him out of her hundred-per-cent eyes. But I do not linger long, because The Sky gets a gander at me, and right away he begins hollering:

'I see before me a sinner of the deepest dye,' he hollers. 'Oh, sinner, repent before it is too late. Join with us, sinner,' he hollers, 'and let us save your soul.'

Naturally, this crack about me being a sinner embarrasses me no little, as it is by no means true, and it is a good thing for The Sky there is no copper in me, or I will go to Mrs. Sky, who is always bragging about how she wins The Sky's soul by outplaying him at his own game, and tell her the truth.

And the truth is that the dice with which she wins The Sky's soul, and which are the same dice with which Brandy Bottle wins all his potatoes, are strictly phony, and that she gets into Nathan Detroit's just in time to keep the Sky from killing old Brandy Bottle.

Frank Loesser

FRANK LOESSER
Caryl Brahms
& Ned Sherrin

It seems to have come as a surprise to many people to learn that Frank Loesser's *Guys and Dolls* is the masterpiece it has always been. Camels have had an easier job getting through the eye of a needle than eager playgoers seeking access to the National Theatre's Olivier auditorium.

Frank Loesser was born in 1910, twenty-two years after Irving Berlin, the other master of music who was equally at home on Broadway and down Tin Pan Alley; but Loesser died in 1969. Berlin was then a vigorous eighty year old and lived on to be a hundred and one before his death in 1989.

Like Berlin, Loesser was weaned on Tin Pan Alley, but again, like Berlin, he discovered that he could write songs for the theatre which sat sunnily on the stage. Indeed, in his handful of shows he was ambitious to stretch and challenge the form of the musical with an instinct for innovation which outstripped Berlin.

He came from a family of serious musicians; his father was a piano teacher and his elder brother, Arthur Loesser, an accomplished pianist and a music critic.

His first song was written at the age of six, the lyric, 'The May Party', celebrated the children's processions he watched in Central Park. At seven he used to listen to the rhythm of the Elevated running through his neighbourhood and put words to it. He ignored his family's encouragement and trained himself, improvising on the piano, composing on the harmonica, and winning third prize in an harmonica contest. His father disapproved of popular songs.

He dropped out of City College after one year. He explained his rejection of a formal musical education by saying, 'I wasn't in the mood to learn.' However, Cynthia Lindsay in her introduction to the *Frank Loesser*

Song Book points out his extraordinary versatility:

He once constructed, with great craftsmanship, the corner (just the corner) of a Regency desk, inlaid and perfectly finished. He then sent it to John Steinbeck, a piece of notepaper attached, with the printed words, *'from the desk of Frank Loesser'*.

His first job was working with words. At eighteen he was briefly employed in New Rochelle, New York, as City Editor on the local newspaper. However, he packed a crash course in song-writing into the early years of the thirties by using his days off to write acts for vaudevillians. Later, he left an account of this period. 'Somehow you had to find a way of getting a job... The Depression was here and I even got one job checking the food and service in a string of restaurants. I was paid seventy-five cents each meal to eat eight or ten meals a day. At least I was eating, which a lot of people weren't. You had to keep alert all the time. I suppose that's where this tremendous energy of mine originated.' Energy he had, explosive energy.

He needed it to cover the range of other jobs he tried in the early thirties, working as a process server, a jewellery salesman, a waiter in a Catskills hotel, and a press agent; and then finally getting a contract to write lyrics for the Leo Fiest music company.

He also landed a job playing and singing at The Back Drop, a night club on 52nd Street, echoed in *Guys and Dolls* as 'The Hot Box'. Finally, he placed five songs in a Broadway revue *The Illustrator's Show*, in 1936, albeit a fiasco. After the show closed, Loesser set off for California and a brief contract with Universal Pictures. It is here that history begins to record Mr. Loesser's eruptions.

The composer, Burton Lane, observed his arrival on the Hollywood scene at a time when musicals were fashionable and, in Hoagy Carmichael's words, 'Everybody was eatin' high on the hog.' Lane was immediately impressed by Loesser's lyrics and arranged for Paramount to give him a contract. In an interview with Max Wilk, Lane vividly evokes the suspense, 'Whilst they were making up their corporate mind whether to sign him on, I had a call from Frank... Could I come over, he wanted to show me some of his work that I hadn't heard. He lived on Sunset Boulevard, I had to walk about two hundred steps down from the street to get to his apartment. I'd been there about five or ten minutes when Lynn, his first wife, asked if I'd like to have dinner with them. I said no, I'd already eaten. She opened a can of beans - one can for both of them - and an apple which she sliced for their dessert. They were absolutely broke... Paramount came through with the contract. A ten-week deal for starters. So I told Frank he could use my office any time. I came in the day after he signed, and I'll never forget this - there was one guy measuring him for shirts, another for shorts, and yet another guy measuring him for suits - the works! The day after he'd signed that contract, everything was going to be made to order.'

Loesser and Lane worked together on a number of pictures for Paramount, and Lane early recognized Loesser's difficult, secretive nature. 'He'd sit across the room from me... and then I'd see him smile... and suddenly he'd jump up and he had it all written out, a complete lyric. I'd put it on my piano and he'd want me to sing it right away. Hell, I hadn't even seen the lyric yet! And if I'd stumble, he'd yell, "God damn it, can't you read ?"'

Hoagy Carmichael remembered Loesser as 'a confident little character swinging his coat-tails and whistling', glimpsed through the window of an office at Paramount. 'I never saw anybody so self-assured.' Loesser was on one of his dozen or so safaris to the commissary for the constant cups of coffee with which he moistened his dogged, lonely, tormented search for appropriate words. 'At first the kid shook me up - his exuberance and zany talk were too much for me.' Carmichael felt that Loesser was insufficiently serious about his craft. He soon found out that this indifference was a front. 'He'd only been joking with me to keep me happy and alive.' Their first song was 'Heart and Soul' which was used in a picture. Then, '... Frank said he wanted to write a song called "Small Fry". I said, "sure", and we did.'

Meanwhile, Loesser was unloading his ideas on a variety of composers.

At Republic Pictures, a considerably less fashionable outfit than Paramount, the music department was run by Cy Feuer, who was later, with Ernest Martin, to produce *Guys and Dolls* , Loesser's biggest success. In 1941 Feuer engaged an all-round musician, vocal coach, rehearsal pianist, choral director and utility conductor, Jule Styne, to do whatever chores were required around the studio. Occasionally, he wrote songs. It was a long time before Jule Styne was to write *Gentlemen Prefer Blondes*, *Funny Girl* or *Gypsy*. His unsubtle first attempt was called 'I Love Watermelon'. 'The man is eating watermelon', explained the director. 'That's what the song has to be about. When a man is sewing a boot and singing, I want him to sing about sewing a boot.' Some months later Republic Pictures grew more ambitious. They were considering investing the, for them, huge sum of half a million dollars in a musical called *Sis Hopkins*. Styne was required to write seven songs. He asked for a good lyric writer - specifically he wanted Frank Loesser, who was being paid two hundred and fifty dollars a week at Paramount. However, his loan-out rate was five hundred. A compromise, which involved trading John Wayne, a Republic star to Universal for a film, was reached, and everyone was happy to accept the explosive Loesser. First he windmilled into Cy Feuer's office, yelling, according to Jule Styne's biographer, 'You son of a bitch, I'm writing for Hoagy Carmichael now. I'm not coming to work with some half-ass piano player who is really a vocal coach.' After two hours of persuasion by Feuer, Loesser agreed at least to talk to Styne. He had not yet agreed to work with him. Feuer recalls that when Loesser was really angry both feet had a tendency to leave the ground. Certainly neither touched the floor when he arrived at Styne's bungalow. The account comes from Theodore Taylor's biography of Styne. 'You have demeaned me by asking for me… ', he shouted, 'you have no respect for my talent, not that I can't understand why you'd want me. But Jesus Christ, every big picture at Paramount they've been giving to Johnny Mercer. Now Goddamit, who writes the hits? Me!' Apart from 'Small Fry' and 'Two Sleepy People', they already included 'I've Got Spurs That Jingle, Jangle, Jingle' and 'Snug as a Bug in a Rug'. Then there were 'Sand In My Shoes' and 'Kiss The Boys Goodbye', written with Victor Schertzinger.

Uncharacteristically, Jule Styne sat silent through Loesser's verbal lashing. Loesser slugged on, 'Now this pile of shit, Republic', he continued, 'you've destroyed me forever.' The fists pounded Styne's desk. 'I'm going to write these f.....g songs in four days; but you're not going to hand them in for three weeks. I'm going to Palm Springs and sit on my butt. You understand that?' Abruptly, Loesser asked Styne to play him something. Styne, at last able to get a word in explained that he had requested Loesser because he wanted to write something good. He began to put his heart on his sleeve. 'I've watched horses shimmy in sync. I've written arrangements for

coyotes, I've written songs about watermelon and guts and gravy... '
Loesser's characteristic menacing pace around the confined space persisted,
and he silenced Styne savagely, 'I don't want your history. I hate your guts.'
Styne started to play a tune, and Loesser's immediate response was to stop
pacing, rush to the door and slam it shut. 'Never play that song here again',
he shouted, and then, modulating to a conspiratorial whisper, 'Don't ever
play that song for anyone else. We'll write that song at Paramount.' 'He was
that kind of schemer', Styne commented in another interview.

Hating the ambience of Republic, Loesser nonetheless worked out his
time there, covering the bungalow office in which they worked with signs
reading 'No Cowboys Allowed, No Horses Allowed, No Gunshots.' He did
not go to Palm Springs or sit on his butt. He continued to fight with Feuer
and even more fiercely with the director of the film; but Styne got used to
his highly individual working methods; the tiny figure pacing and pacing the
small bungalow; listening and listening to a tune over and over again. Never
confiding a lyrical idea until it was fully formed in his mind. As soon as *Sis
Hopkins* was finished, he arranged for Styne to be lent to Universal for
Sweater Girl, and Styne crossed the border without declaring the tune that
had so appealed to Loesser. Loesser took five weeks of anxious
perambulation, smiling mysteriously to himself, drinking from his bottomless
well of coffee and smoking endless
cigarettes while Styne played the song
again and again. At last, with no
warning, Loesser arrived one morning
and said that he was ready to reveal the
lyric - it was 'I Don't Want to Walk
Without You, Baby'.

During his first stay in
Hollywood, Loesser was also to write
with Arthur Schwartz, Jimmy McHugh
and Frederick Hollaender. With
Schwartz he wrote 'They're Either Too
Young or Too Old' for Bette Davis.
With Frederick Hollaender he wrote
the score for *Destry Rides Again*,
including Dietrich's 'See What the

Cy Feuer (left) and
Ernest H. Martin

Boys in the Back Room Will Have'.

Loesser left Hollywood for the army with a characteristic gesture. When Jule Styne asked with whom he should now collaborate Loesser had no hesitation in saying, 'You've been spoiled. There's no one like me... I'll tell you what. If you want someone like me, don't get a clever rhymer, because there's a thing called a rhyming dictionary. Anybody can rhyme, you can find a rhyme for anything. But get a guy who can say something clever and warm, because you need warm lyrics for your music.'

'Warm and clever' is an apt summing up of Loesser's distinctive skill, never better realized than in 'Spring Will Be A Little Late This Year'.

In the forties, Loesser wrote a series of army songs, 'Praise the Lord and Pass the Ammunition' and 'What Do You Do In The Infantry?' among them.

The war in one of its more useful side effects subtly pushed Loesser further along the songwriter's road. For a long time the abrasive little man had been ambitious to write his own music. 'Praise the Lord and Pass the Ammunition' was the first song for which he wrote words and music, and it gave him confidence to experiment further. Loesser's war songs represent the Tin Pan Alley side of his talent; but now it was time for him to start to show his Broadway paces. His first attempt was modest; but fresh and engaging. Feuer and Martin were trying to make their own Broadway debut as producers. Their project was a musical version of the old English farce, *Charley's Aunt*; the new title was *Where's Charley?*

Feuer's first instinct was to team Loesser with Harold Arlen, but when Arlen proved unavailable Feuer and his partner decided to risk Loesser alone. There were a number of people who had to be convinced. First there was the star, Ray Bolger, but Loesser charmed him. Then there were backers to be impressed. Rodgers and Hammerstein, who were familiar with Loesser's

Jo Swerling

music, invested in the show.

In 1948 there was no more potent lure to persuade speculators to throw their money away than to give them a chance to follow Rodgers and Hammerstein up any garden path. George Abbott directed and made a charming leisurely adaptation of the play. Georges Balanchine did the choreography; but it is the range and freshness of Loesser's work which still stands out. He contributed love songs like, 'Once In Love With Amy' and 'My Darling, My Darling', which were very successful, but perhaps the song that points most directly to the innovative qualities for which Loesser's scores were to become famous is the march 'The New Ashmolean Marching Society and Students' Conservatory Band'; it embodies all his relish for setting an amusingly convoluted phrase happily on an irresistible tune as he was later to do with 'some irresponsible dress manufacturer' in *How To Succeed* and 'The Oldest Established Floating Crap Game' in *Guys and Dolls*.

Strangely, *Where's Charley?* was slow to catch on despite congratulatory telegrams from Rodgers and Hammerstein, Cole Porter and countless other composers. Finally, Arthur Schwartz wrote an unsolicited article in the New York Times, stating quite directly that Frank Loesser was, 'the greatest undiscovered composer in America'. It tipped the balance at the box office.

Abe Burrows

Loesser's next show with Feuer and Martin was *Guys and Dolls*. This time he was teamed with Abe Burrows (after an abortive book by Jo Swerling) and the director, George S. Kaufman. He had found the perfect subject, the Broadway world of Damon Runyon and in particular 'The Idyll of Miss Sarah Brown'. Loesser's essence was urban.

Max Wilk quotes Ernest Martin, 'strictly a city boy. Loved to quote Nunnally Johnson, who said that if he had a place with green grass he'd pave it.' Martin has also described Loesser's working habits at this period;

Michael Kidd

they were eccentric to say the least. He rose at around four-thirty or five and made himself a martini. He was not a lush, it simply got him going. He would write from five to eight and then go back to sleep. The stint of sleep would be followed by another three or four hour burst of work and another nap. Friends who he knew were early risers were liable to get six o'clock telephone calls to be treated to his latest work - to paraphrase his lyric, his time of day was the dark time, a couple of bars before dawn. He never agreed formally to write *Guys and Dolls*; the day he handed Feuer and Martin the first four songs was the day they knew they had a show. His eccentricities were Runyonesque. He had a phobia about sitting in public places unless his back was to the wall, and the result of teaming him with Runyon was a perfect marriage.

It was Loesser who threw out Swerling's original book; but perversely he still wrote his score around it. However, his sure theatrical instinct developed so rapidly that Burrows found it possible to construct his new story line writing from song to song. 'I had those songs of Frank's to go by', Burrows told Max Wilk, 'but then we'd sit and we'd look hard for song-spots.' An exception was 'The Fugue for Tin Horns', which seemed to have no place in the plot and so was placed at the opening of the show, wonderfully setting the mood for the play and the exotic world and picturesque vocabulary of the Runyon characters who inhabited it.

Guys and Dolls not only confirmed Loesser's reputation as a songwriter, but also as a volatile colleague. One of his most towering displays of temper came during the first stage rehearsal of The Crap Game number which was interpolated into the show in Philadelphia. Michael Kidd, the choreographer, was starting to stage it when Loesser launched himself at the stage from the back of the stalls in a flurry of four-letter words. He wanted to hear the song loud and perfect every time. In his book, loud was good. Kidd's plea for patience was ignored: Martin's intervention simply increased the fury, 'You're Hitler!... I'm the author and you're working for me!' The rehearsal came to a standstill. The cast came to attention. Motionless at the tops of their voices they bellowed the song; Feuer and Martin saw Loesser backing away up the aisle and followed him out of the theatre where they watched him buy an ice cream and lick it contentedly all the way to his hotel. He had drawn attention to his music and he was happy. He had heard it loud and he had heard it good.

On another occasion, he was rehearsing Isabel Bigley, as Sarah Brown, in a romantic song of considerable range, 'I'll Know'. So infuriated was Loesser by Miss Bigley's inability to perform the song without breaking somewhere in the middle of her register that he leapt on stage and punched her on the nose. Her floods of tears brought him to an awareness of what he had done and from that moment she had the upper hand - and an extremely expensive bracelet to decorate its wrist. The sharp, funny songs, 'A Bushel and a Peck', 'Take Back Your Mink' and 'Adelaide's Lament', came quickly to Loesser, drawing on the idiom and life-style of the crooked but basically soft characters he had met in the thirties while playing piano at The Back Drop.

The romantic songs are not as vivid as the comic numbers, dear though they were to Loesser's heart; but they all comply cleverly with his dictum: character not event.

'I'm in the romance business', Loesser used to yell at Feuer and Martin during the out of town try-outs of *Guys and Dolls*. The argument centred on his wish to reprise ballads in the second act. Finally, George S. Kaufman, the director, and in this case arbitrator, quietened the composer, who was yelling, 'When are they going to hear my songs? What the hell do you think I'm in this for?' by agreeing to reprise Loesser's ballads in the second act if Loesser would allow Kaufman to reprise some of the first act jokes.

Now that Loesser was winning awards his characteristic response each time was an unvarnished, 'I thought I should have won it three years ago.'

His next project was a musical based on Sydney Howard's 1924 play, *They Knew What They Wanted*. He called it *The Most Happy Fella*. This time there were to be no collaborators - he knew what he wanted: to go it alone. There were only fifteen minutes of spoken dialogue. Loesser was working towards an almost operatic form, but he was careful not to say so.

Programme for New York premiere
production, 3 May 1956

On one occasion he called the show 'an extended musical comedy'. On another, he said, 'I may give the impression this show has operatic tendencies. If people feel that way - fine. Actually all it has is a great frequency of songs.' The arranger, Don Walker, phrased it more succinctly. 'This is a musical comedy expanded. Not an opera cut down.' Cynthia Lindsay recalls Loesser quoting George S. Kaufman, 'Of course be corny - just don't let them catch you at it.' So Loesser sneaked what was virtually an opera on to the stage, and they didn't catch him at it. 'The programme simply called it a musical.'

His approach to Howard's play was direct and uncompromising. 'I figured take out all this political talk, the labor talk and the religious talk. Get rid of all that stuff and you have a love story.' In place of the material he had cut he introduced two comedy characters of his own. They provided the laughs - as 'Adelaide' and 'Nathan' had done in *Guys and Dolls*.

It took Loesser four years to write *The Most Happy Fella*. Violent depressions would be followed by bursts of enthusiasm and creativity. He packed his score with more than thirty separate musical numbers.

Choral passages, recitatives, arias, duets, trios, quartets; but this time the
enormous range from vaudeville turns to floridly arioso operatic passages
was not bound together by the same consistent style and tone that Loesser
had found for *Guys and Dolls*.

Perhaps he was more at home in the city. Perhaps the green grass of the
Napa Valley needed to be paved over with Broadway concrete before he
could tread the turf with complete assurance. Perhaps the subject was too
close to him and its central situation too sentimental. Cynthia Lindsay points
out that Loesser, although a deeply sentimental person himself, detested
oversentimentality onstage; he took as his working slogan, 'the heart must
bleed, not slobber'. The degree to which his work matched that motto is the
degree to which *The Most Happy Fella* succeeds.

Whatever the verdict it was a work of prodigal richness. The
conductor, Herbert Green, paints a vivid picture of Loesser in the vortex of
production. 'If you knew Frank Loesser you were involved. You had no
choice, because the man was a genius. Working with him was a mixture of
wanting to kiss him or kill him. Professionally he was unreasonable,
irascible, unfair and infuriating; socially he was gracious, thoughtful, gentle
and totally enchanting - he would find the most miserable looking person at
a party and go and talk to him.'

The New York production of *The Most Happy Fella* ran for a year and
a half; perhaps its flaws can best be summed up in one of its chorus numbers
'Abbondanza! … Che stravaganza'. Loesser was offering an abundance of
abundance.

Stories of his tough business deals were always contrasted with 'funny
stories, outrageous stories, stories of his enormous generosity … there were
the friends who couldn't talk about him without crying, because he was so
many things to so many people and special to each'. In *The Most Happy
Fella* he was too generous to his audience.

In one of Frank Loesser's blocked periods during his work on The
Most Happy Fella, Samuel Goldwyn offered him *Hans Christian Andersen*,
the film, starring Danny Kaye. It was essentially a film for children; but it
provided an alternative National Anthem for the Danes, 'Wonderful
Copenhagen'. It is interesting that when a leaden stage version of *Hans
Christian Andersen* was presented at the London Palladium it did not come
to life. Had Loesser intended his score to be for the theatre, he would have

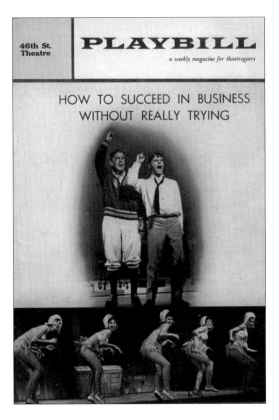

Programme for New York premiere production, 14 October 1961

written it differently. The man who could take on Tin Pan Alley and Broadway certainly understood the difference between the two.

However, in *Greenwillow*, 1960, his next Broadway show, his theatrical instincts were not strong enough to breathe drama into the delicate, fragile folk tale. As Walter Kerr's review said, 'Folklore may be one dish that can't be cooked to order.' Neither the presence of Anthony Perkins in the cast nor a substantial advance could prolong the show's run above three months. Loesser was away in London on the closing night. His cable to the cast, which replaced the usual formal notice, ran, 'Oops - sorry'.

Next time, his feet were firmly back on the asphalt. *How To Succeed in Business Without Really Trying* was a satire on big corporations which provided him with an urban environment almost as mannered and much more identifiable than the Runyonesque fantasy of *Guys and Dolls*.

Rudy Vallee making his first Broadway appearance since *George White's Scandals of 1936*, inspired another of Loesser's epic rages. Vallee did not want to perform one of his songs the way Loesser had written it. 'I am an interpreter of songs', was his point of view. Correctly, the producers stuck to the principle that the creator's instinct must be served and Loesser got his way; but not before he had fired off a telegram two pages long arguing that Feuer and Martin had betrayed him by not punching Vallee firmly on the nose. Shades of Isabel Bigley!

Throughout the show, Loesser rigorously followed his dictum, 'Remember a song is like a freight train moving across a stage. Every boxcar has a word on it. These people have to hear everything and understand it - fast, because in a minute the car will be gone and they'll never see it again. Make them listen and then lay it in their laps.' They listened to *How To Succeed* for 1,416 performances on Broadway; and it joined the select band of American musicals to be awarded a Pulitzer Prize.

Loesser worked on one more musical, *Pleasures and Palaces*, which closed out of town, sunk it would appear, by its book.

He was a genuine original, and an innovator, not in the sense that he came to the musical theatre with a considered statement of what he felt it should achieve; but with a pragmatic assurance about what he could make it do for him. His business enterprises were as time-consuming as his creative work. His music publishing company developed and encouraged young writers, notably Adler and Ross, who wrote *Pajama Game* and *Damn Yankees*; Meredith Willson, who wrote *The Music Man* and, in England, Peter Greenwell, the composer of *Twenty Minutes South*, *The Crooked Mile* and *The Mitford Girls*.

A strange, contentious, ebullient, ambitious, gifted man - a street boy, always with a deal in his mind, a felicitous phrase in his soul and his eye on the stars; a genius entitled to his own assessment that he had it.

He died of lung cancer at the age of fifty-nine on 28 July 1969, a breathing machine on one side of him, a packet of cigarettes on the other.

Vivian Blaine

HALF A CENTURY OF
GUYS AND DOLLS

Matt Wolf

Guys and Dolls, Frank Loesser's immortal 1950 musical, is a Broadway paradox. More than any other musical with the possible exception of *West Side Story*, the show embodies the quintessence of New York, despite being a self-described 'musical fable' – New York as we wish it were, not as it ever was – drawn from the stories of Kansas-born Damon Runyon, who himself didn't even arrive in Manhattan until he was 26. Three of the four original principals were making their Broadway debuts, and the fourth, Sam Levene , had never done a musical before. The director, George S. Kaufman, was a celebrated playwright with no musical experience.

Still, it's in the nature of Broadway to work its magic in unexpected ways, and *Guys and Dolls* arrived at the 46th Street Theatre from Philadelphia trailing out-of-town bouquets. The creative team was the result of careful attention on the part of producers Cy Feuer and Ernest Martin, who were collaborating on their second show with Loesser, following the composer's Broadway debut with *Where's Charley?* in 1948. But if that show took as its source an 1892 English farce, *Charley's Aunt*, the new musical needed to be a high-style celebration of low-life New York, rooted in the Runyon short story, 'The Idyll of Miss Sarah Brown'. The producers were emboldened by the success the previous season of *South Pacific*; after all, if Nellie Forbush and Emile de Becque could make a winning Broadway couple, why couldn't Sky Masterson and Sarah Brown?

Hollywood screenwriter Jo Swerling was the first librettist, though 10 others were brought in to rewrite the book before the producers decided upon radio script writer Abe Burrows, a New Yorker making his Broadway debut. (Among Burrows' takeoffs on popular song writing had been such titles as 'Morning Becomes Electra, But You Look Better At Night'.) Burrows' brief was to fashion a ripely comic scenario that could be fitted to Loesser's (by then) pre-existing score, since the composer had finished his work before Burrows even came on board.

Immediately, Burrows' keen intelligence reaped rewards: it was he who decided Miss Adelaide should catch her defining cold not from a nightclub strip-tease but as a psychosomatic response to a 14-year engagement to Nathan Detroit with no end in sight. That the Loesser-Burrows partnership was a fruitful one was to be proven again eleven years later, when their 1961 *How To Succeed In Business Without Really Trying* was awarded the Pulitzer Prize.

The 24 November 1950 opening elicited the kinds of raves that this show uniquely seems to call forth. 'Gusty and uproarious,' wrote Brooks Atkinson in the New York Times, praising the technical aspects of the production as 'a work of art'. – Michael Kidd's choreography included, from its opening pantomime ballet onwards. Wrote the Daily News' John Chapman: 'The big trouble is that a performance of *Guys and Dolls* lasts only one evening when it ought to last about a week. I did not want to leave the theatre.'

At last, the Damon Runyon preserved on screen in *Little Miss Marker*, with Shirley Temple , and *Lady For A Day*, with May Robson , had made it to the stage. His was a world where inveterate gambling was 'evil,' but where no reprobate was too far gone that a rousing eleventh-hour number, and the attentions of a doll, couldn't put him right.

The production won Tonys for Robert Alda (father of Alan), as Sky Masterson, and Isabel Bigley as Sarah Brown, as well as for direction, choreography, and the show itself. Only the presence that season of *Call Me Madam* served to prevent a *Guys and Dolls* sweep: the Irving Berlin show won for best score and gave Ethel Merman the best actress Tony that would otherwise surely have gone to Hollywood star Vivian Blaine, whose adenoidal Miss Adelaide launched her as a most welcome Broadway debutante.

The show ran for 1,200 performances, was sold to films for $1 million, and signalled the zenith of the New York theatre's favourite art form. The first national tour ran over two years, with Allan Jones (Sky), Pamela

Britton (Adelaide), Jan Clayton (Sarah), and Julie Oshins (Nathan), and various New York revivals – usually short summer runs at City Centre or Theatre-In-the-Park – in 1955, 1959, and 1966 boasted such names as Walter Matthau (the '55 Nathan), Lloyd Bridges (the '59 Sky), and, in '66, the return of Vivian Blaine to what became her signature role in the theatre.

In 1976, Broadway producer Moe Septee opened an all-black revival of *Guys and Dolls* at the Broadway Theatre, boasting several members of the team that had brought Septee's previous *Bubbling Brown Sugar* a Tony nomination for Best Musical: Danny Holgate (orchestrator/arranger), Bernard Johnson (costume designer), and Billy Wilson (director/choreographer). The production ran 239 performances and got a Tony nomination for the Nathan of Robert Guillaume, star of the American television show *Benson*. Most people's memories, though, were of the Nicely-Nicely Johnson of Ken Page, a huge-voiced Broadway butterball not dissimilar in appeal to Clive Rowe in the 1996 London revival, and of Ernestine Jackson's Sister Sarah: two sterlingly sung performances in an evening that managed for the most part to replace Jewishness with jive. Its upbeat arrangements, though, fell foul of Jo Sullivan Loesser, the composer's widow. A keen guardian of her late husband's estate, Mrs. Loesser wasn't wild about the staging and to this day won't allow Holgate's jazzed-up orchestrations to be played.

Programme for 'all-black' *Guys and Dolls*, New York 1976.

The most recent Broadway hurrah of *Guys and Dolls* came in 1992 in a $5.5 million revival that opened on 14 April at the Martin Beck Theatre. (Interestingly, the film 37 years earlier cost exactly the same amount.) Directed by Jerry Zaks, the production survived a bumpy preview period – its Sister Sarah, Carolyn Mignini, was fired and replaced by understudy Josie de Guzman – to garner a set of reviews that eclipsed even the

'Sue Me': Sam Levene (Nathan) and Vivian Blaine (Adelaide), London 1953.

originals. As was true the first time, it was the Adelaide – Faith Prince – who became the reviewers' darling, though Peter Gallagher and Nathan Lane, as Sky and Nathan, got their ample share of raves. (Lane, indeed, owes his first name to the musical, since he chose it while appearing as Nathan Detroit in a New Jersey dinner theatre production at the age of 21.)

'The cherished Runyonland of memory is not altered, just felt and dreamt anew by intoxicated theatre artists,' enthused the New York Times' Frank Rich. Echoed New York Magazine's John Simon: 'This *Guys and Dolls* is permanently floating and you'll swing with it like a bell' – two song references in one sentence. The production won four Tony Awards, including best revival, and managed to lift the stigma surrounding revivals that had long prevailed on Broadway. Unlike the embalmed 1987 Broadway revival of *Cabaret*, with Joel Grey, Zaks showed you could release an energy and dynamism synonymous with Broadway by rethinking a show for now while honouring what made it great then: certainly it was better sung and danced than the original could have been, especially since that first Nathan of Sam Levene was famous for not being able to sing a note.

Running 1144 performances, just 56 fewer than the original, the production spawned a national tour starring Lorna Luft (Liza Minnelli's half-sister) and proved to be no mere revival; Zaks' *Guys and Dolls* was one of those banner events trumpeting a revitalised Broadway, and its feel-good effect on morale was evident up and down the Street. You can bet it will be years before any New York producer tackles the show again.

The film of *Guys and Dolls*, directed by Joseph L. Mankiewicz, was released in 1955, but despite a cast that looked great on paper it was a very partial success. Loesser had reservations about the movie, and who could blame him, since it cut two of the best songs in the show – 'A Bushel and A Peck' and 'I've Never Been In Love Before' – and cast as Nathan Frank Sinatra, who was a much more obvious Sky. Sinatra did, however, get to sing 'Adelaide', a Loesser melody written specifically for the film.

Instead, notwithstanding lobbying from Gene Kelly to play the part, Marlon Brando played Sky opposite Jean Simmons' Sarah, and was given a new number, 'A Woman In Love'. Vivian Blaine was retained as Adelaide, a role for which Betty Grable had busily put herself forward, as were Broadway originals Stubby Kaye, Johnny Silver, and B.S. Pully, repeating their performances as Nicely-Nicely, Benny Southstreet, and Big Jule, respectively. In the end, the film was nominated for an Oscar for 'scoring of a musical picture,' without – amazingly – getting a single citation for best song. (Loesser had won the Best Song Oscar in 1949 for 'Baby, It's Cold Outside', from *Neptune's Daughter*.) It was left to *The King and I* the following year to show how a Broadway classic might be reinvented on screen.

The show's English history is an unusual one. The 1953 British premiere at the Coliseum, where the musical played 555 performances, was essentially a reproduction of its Broadway forebear. Vivian Blaine and Sam Levene (as well as Stubby Kaye and, as Harry the Horse, Tom Pedi) repeated their performances, joined by Lizbeth Webb (Sarah) and Jerry Wayne (Sky). The opening prompted an anticipatory fever not felt by an American musical in London since *Oklahoma!* at Drury Lane in 1947.

As it happened, the reviews were decidedly mixed, though perhaps no more so than any Broadway success that travels to London, since British critics revel in trumping their New York colleagues. While the Evening Standard (Kenneth Tynan) thought the show 'not only a young masterpiece but the Beggar's Opera of Broadway' and The Times called it 'a wonderful evening,' the Daily Mail found the music to be 'its main weakness' (!) and at least one Sunday paper spoke of the show 'deserving its first-night collapse' – a reference to booing from the gallery and of a chauvinism championing local girl Lizbeth Webb over Vivian Blaine or, for that matter, any Broadway interloper.

Still, the musical eventually entered the English repertoire of American greats, and was produced around the country – at Leicester in 1975, directed by Robin Midgley, and at the Palace Theatre, Watford, the following year, with Benny Lee as Nathan and an American unknown called Clarke Peters as Sky. East London's Half Moon Theatre attempted a miniaturised revival, performed by a vastly reduced cast. Long before that, over at the National, Laurence Olivier had long been wanting to play Nathan opposite Geraldine McEwan's Adelaide, having been encouraged by Kenneth Tynan to bring a musical within the NT repertoire; Garson Kanin was to cross the Atlantic to direct. Instead, the production was scuppered twice, once by illness (Olivier's thrombosis), the second time by the worrying economies of mounting such a large-scale musical at such a (relatively) small venue as the Old Vic.

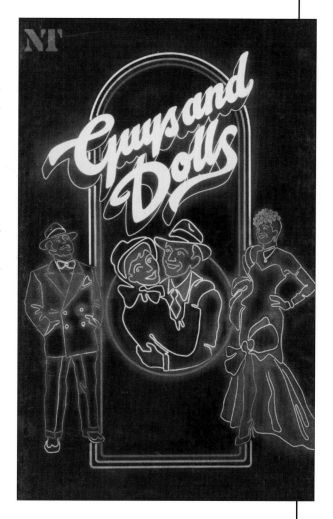

nter Richard Eyre in 1982. A newly appointed NT associate director who had directed films for the BBC and social realist plays by new writers around Britain, Eyre chose for his South Bank debut a musical with which he had become reacquainted when stumbling upon the original cast album in a Soho record shop. Budgeted then at less than £200,000, the aim was to end the apartheid between practitioners of musicals and those of plays by marrying the two within a subsidised context devoted to the truthful examination of text. The point was that *Guys and Dolls* was among the few musicals that could withstand such an approach, since it was as densely and tightly written as a first-rate play and as pungently hermetic in its Runyonesque way as the worlds of Flann O'Brien and P.G. Wodehouse were in theirs. But whether the press and public would go for such an experiment was another matter; if *Guys and Dolls* were to fail, it would fail very, very publicly.

The production opened on 9 March 1982, with Julie Covington – the first person Eyre cast – and Julia McKenzie playing distaff partners to Ian Charleson and Bob Hoskins, all of them singing and dancing away next to an onstage band. (It was to be Hoskins' last stage work for 14 years before he followed the fold of the cinema.) And while the word from previews ranged from encouraging to ecstatic, the critics made the buzz official. 'The National has blown up my apprehensions and done an exhilarating job,' said John Barber in the Daily Telegraph. Wrote the Spectator's Mark Amory: 'The production is a smash hit, and deserves to be.'

And so it was. The show won five Olivier Awards; sold 393,926 seats over two-and-a-half years to play to 95% capacity; and proved an invaluable repertory asset when a subsequent Olivier musical, *Jean Seberg*, closed on

Programme for National Theatre revival, London 1982.

43

4 April 1984, after a truncated four-month run, allowing *Guys and Dolls* to be brought back. A West End engagement, starring Lulu, Norman Rossington, Betsy Brantley, and Clarke Peters, opened on 19 June 1985 at the Prince of Wales's for a nine-month run. Its director – Richard Eyre being away filming *Tumbledown* for the BBC – was Antonia Bird, who would go on to direct such acclaimed films as *Priest*. All told, after recoupment of costs the production contributed nearly £1 million to the NT and kept the theatre's parlous finances in the early '80s from the brink of disaster.

Prompted no doubt by the NT's success, the musical became a repertory regular up and down the country – at The Belgrade Theatre, Coventry, in 1987; the Forum Theatre, Wythenshawe, in 1989 (Kelly Hunter, co-star of the ill-fated *Jean Seberg*, played Adelaide, with Janie Dee as Sarah); and at the Leicester Haymarket in 1988, co-directed by Peter Lichtenfels and Tim Supple, and again in 1995 (in association with Dublin's Gaiety Theatre), directed by Paul Kerryson. Come Christmas 1996, and the National found itself with a hole in its holiday repertoire, which got Richard Eyre thinking one day as he manoeuvred a wheelbarrow in his garden: Could luck be a lady twice?

Which is where our story begins.

BROADWAY 1950

Stanley Green

Though it turned out to be one of Broadway's most hilarious musical comedies - as well as an acknowledged classic in the field - *Guys and Dolls* was originally planned as a serious romantic story. Much impressed by the success of *South Pacific*, producers Cy Feuer and Ernest Martin felt that if such a compelling musical play could be written about the unlikely romance between naive Nellie Forbush and sophisticated Emile de Becque, an equally affecting story could be created out of the unlikely romance between a pure-at-heart Salvation Army-type reformer and a slick Broadway gambler, the two leading characters in Damon Runyon's short story 'The Idyll of Miss Sarah Brown.' For the score, the producers enlisted Frank Loesser (with whom they had been associated on *Where's Charley?*), then tried some 11 librettists though none came up with an acceptable script. The last of these writers, Jo Swerling, had a contract giving him primary credit as author no matter how many subsequent changes might be made, which is the reason why his name always appears on programmes as co-librettist. After so many script rejections, Feuer and Martin changed their minds and now decided that *Guys and Dolls* could only work if it were played for laughs. This led them to Abe Burrows, a radio and television comedy writer without theatrical experience, who wrote an entirely new book that he fitted to Loesser's already existing score.

Programme for New York premiere production, It opened on 24 November 1950 and ran for 1,194 performances.

In this so-called 'Musical Fable of Broadway,' the high-minded lowlifes and spunky do-gooders of Damon Runyon's world come colorfully alive in such characters as Sky Masterson (Robert Alda), the bet-on-anything gambler; Nathan Detroit (Sam Levene), the perpetually harried organizer of the oldest established permanent floating crap game in New York, who bets Sky that he can't make the next girl he sees fall in love with him; Miss Sarah Brown (Isabel Bigley) of the Save-A-Soul Mission on Times Square, who is the next girl Sky sees and who does succumb; and Miss Adelaide (Vivian Blaine), the main attraction at the Hot Box nightclub, whose psychosomatic perpetual cold stems from her being engaged to Nathan for 14 years. One of the show's memorable scenes occurs in the mission where Nicely-Nicely Johnson (Stubby Kaye) confesses his sins in the rousing 'Sit Down, You're Rockin' The Boat.' *Guys and Dolls* was the fifth longest-running Broadway musical of the Fifties.

Programme for New York premiere production, after Martha Stewart had replaced Vivian Blaine.

LONDON 1953

Kenneth Tynan

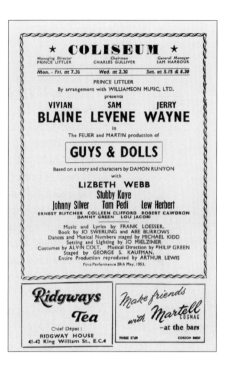

*G*uys and Dolls, at which I am privileged to take a peek last evening, is a hundred-per-cent American musical caper, cooked up out of a story called 'The Idyll of Miss Sarah Brown', by the late Damon Runyon, who is such a scribe as delights to give the English language a nice kick in the pants.

This particular fable takes place in and around Times Square in New York City, where many citizens do nothing but roll dice all night long, which is held by one and all, and especially the gendarmes, to be a great vice. Among the parties hopping around in this neighbourhood is a guy by the name of Nathan Detroit, who operates a floating dice game, and Miss Adelaide, his ever-loving pretty, who is sored up at this Nathan because after fourteen years' engagement, they are still nothing but engaged. Anyway, being short of ready scratch, Nathan lays a bet with a large gambler called Sky Masterson, the subject of the wager being whether The Sky can talk a certain Salvation Army doll into joining him on a trip to Havana. Naturally, Nathan figures that a nice doll such as this will die sooner, but by and by she and The Sky get to looking back and forth at each other, and before you know it she is his sweet-pea. What happens next but The Sky gets bopped by religion and shoots craps with Nathan and the boys for their immortal souls. And where do the sinners wind up, with their chalk-striped suits and busted noses, but at a prayer meeting in the doll's mission house, which hands me a very big laugh indeed. The actors who nab the jobs of playing these apes and essences of 42nd Street have me all tuckered out with clapping them.

Nathan Detroit is Sam Levene, who expostulates very good with his arms, which are as long as a monkey's. Stubby Kaye, who plays Nicely-Nicely Johnson, the well-known horse-player, is built on lines which are by no means dinky, for his poundage maybe runs into zillions, but he gives with a voice which is as couth as a choir boy's or maybe couther. He

Programme for London premiere production, 28 May 1953. It ran for 555 performances.

commences the evening by joining in a three-part comedy song about the nags. In fact, it is a fugue, and I will give you plenty of eleven to five that it is the first fugue many patrons of the Coliseum ever hear. Miss Vivian Blaine (Miss Adelaide) is a very choice blonde judy and she gets to sing a song which goes as follows: 'Take back your mink to from whence it came' and which hits me slap-dab in the ear as being supernaturally comical. Myself, I prefer her to Miss Lizbeth Webb, who plays the mission doll, but, naturally, I do not mention such an idea out loud.

The Coliseum is no rabbit hutch, and maybe a show as quick and smart as this *Guys and Dolls* will go better in such a sized theatre as the Cambridge Theatre. Personally, I found myself laughing ha-ha last night more often than a guy in the critical dodge has any right to. And I am ready to up and drop on my knees before Frank Loesser, who writes the music and lyrics. In fact, this Loesser is maybe the best light composer in the world. In fact, the chances are that *Guys and Dolls* is not only a young masterpiece, but the Beggar's Opera of Broadway.

'Guys and Dolls': Stubby Kaye (Nicely-Nicely), George Baron (a Guy), Johnny Silver (Benny) and Pamela Devis (a Doll) in the London premiere.

Hollywood 1955

Life Magazine

Famous musical becomes stylish movie

Showmanship, frequently associated with making a dubious product look good to the public, is rarely employed in lending more gilt to an already gilt-edged property. But in making a movie out of *Guys and Dolls*, the Broadway musical classic that ran two and a half years in New York, old Hollywood Showman Sam Goldwyn has left no stunt unturned. First he paid its producers and authors a whopping million dollars (plus ten percent of the world gross) for the rowdy extravaganza. Then, to play the oddly assorted rough diamonds created by writer Damon Runyon he hired an expensive quartet of stars. Finally he spent another fortune rounding up an expert directing, designing, composing and choreographic staff - and revived the old Goldwyn reputation for pretty show girls.

All the effort and money - $5.5 million out of Goldwyn's own pocket since he has never taken outside backing for his films - has been well spent. The movie *Guys and Dolls*, like its enormously successful stage predecessor, is a stylish, ear-filling film with notable surprises in it. Fast-moving and often exciting, it should pay off its eminent backer quite handsomely - in the words of the late Damon Runyon himself, a good deal more than somewhat.

The two biggest gambles Goldwyn took in *Guys* are the ones that pay off the biggest. As the hero he cast Marlon Brando, who had never sung a note or danced a step in a movie. As the heroine he picked Jean Simmons, who, though she had sung in a British film, had never been in a real musical.

Brando is wonderful as Broadway rogue Sky Masterson, singing with an ingratiating, convincing baritone - his own, as promised. But it is Simmons who almost runs away with the movie. Playing Sarah Brown, the prim Save-a-Soul mission worker who falls for the rogue, she unveils a sweet lyric soprano and, in a gaudy nightclub brawl, uncorks a mannish clout that is the sensation of the film.

Marlon Brando as Sky and Jean Simmons as Sarah

THE 'TIME OUT' FILM GUIDE

Tom Milne

GUYS AND DOLLS

(Joseph L. Mankiewicz, 1955, US)
Marlon Brando, Jean Simmons, Frank Sinatra,
Vivian Blaine, Stubby Kaye, Robert Keith.
150 min.

A musical fairly glittering with intelligence and invention. Too much talk, its critics said (not for the first time with Mankiewicz). But quite apart from the fact that much of this talk is delectable Runyonese, some defence is necessary against the frenzied brilliance of Michael Kidd's choreography, which threatens to deluge the screen in energy and eccentricity right from the pyrotechnic opening number that establishes the teeming underworld of Times Square. Relaxed and caressing, the dialogue sequences serve as a kind of foreplay, enhancing not merely the exquisite eruptions of pleasure aroused by the musical numbers, but the genuine lyricism of the romance between gambler Sky Masterson and his Salvation Army doll. Inspired casting here, with Brando and Simmons - a Method counterbalance to the more traditional showbiz coupling of Sinatra and Blaine - lending an emotional depth rare in musicals.

Finale of National Theatre revival, re-cast 12 April 1984.

LONDON 1982

Russell Davies

'**W**hy,' ran the eternal question before this production opened, 'should our National Theatre be doing an American musical, a hit from the commercial stage?' Even at the time, there were ready answers to this, such as 'Why shouldn't they?' and 'In the cultural climate most of us hope for, there will scarcely be any such thing as the uncommercial stage.' But the sight of the thing being done, on the broad apron of the Olivier, has banished theory in any case. *Guys and Dolls* is a terrific show, performed really well, and those who would rather it hadn't happened are revealed as wet blankets of the soggiest kind.

The process wouldn't have worked with any old musical. A National Theatre *Oklahoma!* would necessarily have turned out as corn-fed pastiche with outbursts of lumbering 'sincerity'. But because *Guys and Dolls* is openly and profoundly a low-life pastiche to begin with, it doesn't even matter that we realize the performers are not native Americans. In fact this enhances the affection in which we hold the show (which is not too stale an affection either, because there are some fine neglected numbers in the score). The first neon signs that come warmly roasting into view to establish the Manhattan landscape (settings: John Gunter, lighting: David Hersey) are 'Wrigley's Spearmint' and 'Maxwell House Coffee' - which suggest a comforting overlap of economies, if not of cultures, between ourselves and Damon Runyon's zoot-suited metropolis.

Barrie Rutter (Benny), Bob Hoskins (Nathan) and David Healy
(Nicely-Nicely) in the 1982 National Theatre revival.

Vocally, we get the same overlap from the cast. After hard work, the accents throughout are a most honourable near-miss. Only Julia McKenzie as Miss Adelaide truly strikes the ear as a possible American import, and she has the advantage of the kind of song ('a poissun can develop a cold') that practically can't be sung except in Pungent Brooklynese. Bill Paterson, as Harry the Horse, has his own solution, a nasal delivery suggesting Walter Matthau in an adenoids crisis. It took time to work Harry out - a pleasant occupation even if Richard Eyre's hot-foot direction didn't leave you many spare moments in which to indulge it.

But it was the way Paterson moved that gave the real clue to the evening's success. This Harry the Horse doesn't walk, he treads - in a rubber-soled, bent-kneed, interior-sprung manner drawn straight from the early American comic papers and animated films. And looking around the ensemble, one realized that everybody had some speciality of this kind going for him. Larrington Walker, to take a single example, was a one-man Harlem at all times. I mean no slight on the dancing profession when I say that the one giant strength of this production was that everything was done by actors. Gone - completely gone - was any sense that a stiff-backed phalanx of principals was being eased through the strenuous part of the evening by a lithe *corps de ballet*. This is an authentic all-singing, all-dancing cast, and though everyone isn't equally good at everything, they're aiming to be, and they all count. The sense of unity achieved by David Toguri's staging was an exhilaration and a delight.

A programme note records Runyon as saying 'To Hell with plots.' People, he claimed, 'remember the characters.' This is certainly true of *Guys and Dolls*, whose plot could be comfortably inscribed on half a postage stamp. Almost its only working part is the bet contracted between Nathan Detroit and Sky Masterson, as to whether the suave, high-rolling Sky from Colorado (nice vocal distinction by Ian Charleson) will persuade Sarah the Salvation Army girl to accompany him on a binge/spree in Havana. Possibly because the process of theatre-going is in several respects emotionally akin to betting - as a show progresses one is constantly placing one's metaphorical money on the characters and shifting the investment about - the audience takes to this gladly, and requires little else in the way of propulsion through the two-and-three-quarter hour show.

But there is plenty of extra gas, and it comes direct from the music. Astonishingly - well, I wasn't aware of it - there are no weak numbers in *Guys and Dolls*. If there is a weakness in the apportioning of Frank Loesser's songs, it's that Nathan Detroit's musical share doesn't match his part in the plot; but this may have come as a relief to Bob Hoskins, whose singing isn't the best of him. Raucous even when *sotto voce*, he is very fine in the dramatic sequences, and probably the only member of the cast whose shape actually justifies a double-breasted suit. David Healy's Nicely-Nicely Johnson wears a perpetual beaming smile that isn't all the role. This is the very picture of an actor seizing, successfully, the part he was built for (come to think of it, I take it all back about Hoskins's exclusive right to The Suit).

Charleson's Sky, a Gary Cooper-style Western hero in better-draped civvies, rises to the songs with unexpected relish, and the climactic note he supplies to 'Luck Be a Lady' tops off the superbly-set sewer encounter in the only appropriate way. He also blends very affectingly with Julie Covington in 'I've Never Been in Love Before', the first-half closer - and this is a stroke of luck, because Miss Covington's voice is of such a special timbre (described by a perceptive admirer as 'like celery') that she isn't easily matched. Hers is easily the toughest role of the night: Sarah is the only character hinting at emotional depth. The plot dictates that her early entrances should put a damper on the gamblers' cavortings, which doesn't make it easier for her to establish herself; but she has nothing to worry about. The Havana scene - brilliantly stoked up by the opening solo from Bobby Orr at the drums - sets her free for what is, in the circumstances, a heroically thoughtful performance. The blend with Julia McKenzie, in their pre-closer 'Marry the Man Today', is again excellent. Miss McKenzie of course, given a whole evening's opportunity to send up her own piercingly traditional skill in the old show-stopper game, is on a winner from the start. I thought there were moments when both ladies would have been helped by some lusher musical upholstery, but the decision not to have strings was apparently forced by budgetary considerations. It did leave the orchestrations leaning sometimes a bit too close to the Brechtian wind-band tradition.

Everyone agrees that *Guys and Dolls* is a 'perfectly efficient mechanism', but there is heart in it too. The book is full of gags that work, or woik ('His wife's havin' a baby. He's noivous, it's his foist wife'), and songs that

Bob Hoskins (Nathan), David Healy (Nicely-Nicely) and Ian Charleson (Sky)
in the 1982 National Theatre revival

are more various, musically, than anyone has a right to expect from a single source. Justice is done to the original author's style ('Take back your mink to from whence it came'), and though the tale is determinedly simple-minded, the talents of our National actors are nevertheless stretched in all available directions. I don't ask for anything more, apart from the chance of buying some more tickets.

BROADWAY 1992

From first read-through to first night

Marty Bell

t's 11a.m. on Monday 27 January 1992, and there are seventy-five people eating bagels and drinking coffee in Studio 4-3, the largest rehearsal hall at 890 Broadway. When you see a crowd of people having bagels and coffee on Monday morning in this building, it's safe to assume it's the first day of rehearsal for a new show. Everyone who will perform any function on the production usually comes to this celebration for a nosh, a peek at a model of the set, and a first read-through of the script. The next time they will all come together will be a very nervous time for all - opening night. But today they get to share a joyous hour since there is nothing yet in the way of hope.

This morning's gathering is particularly giddy since what this collection of actors, creative staff, producers, and production staff is about to tackle is perhaps the most beloved American musical of all time, *Guys and Dolls*. My hunch is that if I took a survey of this room, I'd find that almost everyone here has done this show at some other point in his or her life - at camp, at school, at church, at shul, at some theatre somewhere. But it's a safe bet that none of them has ever done it in the way they're about to - as an in-your-face, ultra-$5 million-plus Broadway extravaganza. We all feel uneasy about the cost of doing Broadway musicals and the resultant high ticket prices, but it does permit a quality of production that simply cannot be found anywhere else.

One thing these folks know they don't have to worry about is getting the script right: the Abe Burrows-Jo Swerling libretto and Frank Loesser score are about as right as they come. This is comforting. It will save a lot of time (and thus, a lot of money) in rehearsal, which, for a new show, is often devoted to working on moments, scenes, and songs that end up cut from the finished piece that eventually opens. On the other hand, it puts an additional pressure on this production. A new show can be 'just good enough' and be successful. But to do a *great* show well is a disappointment. A great show must be done great to really be a success. To that end, Dodger Productions, the producing office consisting of Michael David, Sherman Warner, and Ed Strong, which took the lead on this production, has approached it as if it is a fresh, new show rather than a shopworn revival. Most revivals of the classic musicals that come to New York (often after being out on the road for a while) are produced with the attitude that the popularity of the material will carry the evening and you can skimp on the production elements. Most of those shows - with the exception of those with a big-name star like Yul Brynner, Anthony Quinn, or, most recently, Tyne Daly - do not recoup their initial investments. But there will be no skimping this time out - even though the $5.5 million investment target has still not been fully reached as of today. Yet, money that can afford the highest quality does not always produce it.

When all those here cluster in front of the windows for a group photograph, the four actors whose names will appear above the show's title - Faith Prince, Nathan Lane, Peter Gallagher, and Carolyn Mignini - sit in the centre of the first row, but leave a middle chair vacant. That seat is soon taken by the man who will ultimately be responsible for the fate of this production: director Jerry Zaks. Most of the pressure is on him. Even if it wasn't, he'd take it upon himself. Zaks, with his wire-rimmed glasses and toothsome omnipresent smile, is funny, fast-talking, enthusiastic, open in the way that people who have been through years of therapy tend to be, and is generally known as a great guy. But he will tell you, 'The "Mr. Nice Guy" thing makes me laugh. People have no idea how ruthless I am in pursuit of making a show work.'

With the deaths of Gower Champion, Michael Bennett, and Bob Fosse in the 1980s, and with Harold Prince continuing to pursue the kind of adventurous work that is only sometimes commercially successful, Zaks has come to share a reputation with Tommy Tune as the only dependable hitmakers in town. Part of this is certainly due to Zaks's and Tune's talents. And part of it is due to the nature of the material they are drawn to - material that fits what they do best.

Zaks will rarely attend a reading or a presentation; he prefers to consider shows submitted in script form. He claims he will do a comedy only if it makes him laugh out loud while he is reading it… Zaks has reason to be confident his sense of humour is shared with a large audience, given his commercial success with his productions of John Guare's *The House of*

Blue Leaves and *Six Degrees of Separation*, Ken Ludwig's *Lend Me a Tenor*, Chris Durang's *Sister Mary Ignatius Explains It All for You*, Larry Shue's *The Foreigner*, and his reworking of the 1934 musical *Anything Goes*. If a script is funny, he's the first director to whom any producer in town will show it... .

'Why don't we get started,' Zaks says, following the photo opportunity. 'I can't believe I am actually saying that.' ... The cast sits in a semicircle of folding chairs on one side of him, and everyone else is in a semicircle on the other side.

'I've been looking forward to this day for a long time,' Zaks tells his company. 'And now that I'm here I want to get to work. I'm not going to bore you with how much I love this show and how precious it is and how much responsibility we all share to do it well. I don't want to scare us to death. I just want to do it.'

Then the charming and soft-spoken scenic designer Tony Walton, with whom Zaks collaborates frequently, holds up his one-inch-to-a-foot scale

Faith Prince (Adelaide) and Nathan Lane (Nathan) in Jerry Zaks's revival, which opened at the Martin Beck Theatre, New York, on 14 April 1992.

models of the set, scene by scene. His approach is a homage to Jo Mielziner's designs for the original 1950 production that opened at the Forty-sixth Street Theatre on Broadway. It is a fantasy Times Square, largely painted on drops, using Walton's own palette of bright pastels. The only suggestion of the scenery now in the rehearsal hall is two wooden, ceiling-high spiral towers that will be necessary for choreographer Chris Chadman to stage the famous crap game in the sewer.

'This show is a great play with great music,' Zaks says. 'And there's something about Tony's scheme that will let the play part play.

'Enough yak-yak-yak. The show that really knocked me out way back when was *Wonderful Town*. All I remember is the light and colour and music exploding out of the proscenium. That's what this is going to be. This set is our world. This set is where our magic is going to take place. It's the vessel that will allow all this to happen. Now I'll stop yakking and let's read it.'

The cast sits with scripts in hand and reads through the show's dialogue. When a song cue arrives, musical director Eddie Strauss plunks out a few bars of the songs everyone knows on the upright piano almost as a tease. The role of Arvide Abernathy, the elderly bass drum player in the Save-A-Soul mission band, has not been cast yet. It's been offered to comic actor Eddie Bracken, but no deal has been made. So Zaks reads that role. His enthusiasm is infectious. His laughter leads the way... After the read-through, the cast takes a break and Zaks sends all but the actors and the production team away. He's content with what he's heard.

'There are no surprises except seeing how far along some people are,' he says. 'They understand the music of the words.'

And he's happy with the collection of character actors he's assembled. 'This is the perfect New York show,' he says. 'It grows out of the fabric of the city. You don't want a lot of white-bread beauty. You need characters. The problem with the movie of this was that those actors weren't these characters, they were pretending to be. But onstage, you just have to find these people.'

Directing is about making choices and having the ability to articulate those choices clearly so your collaborators can execute them. In several meetings between the first day of rehearsal and the week after the opening of *Guys and Dolls*, Jerry Zaks sat in his office above the Jujamcyn organization's headquarters and discussed his job, and the decisions he was faced with - big and small - that went into the show. The very first decision a director must make, of course, is whether or not to do a specific show...

The possibility of directing *Guys and Dolls* was first brought up in 1989 when Zaks was director-in-residence at Lincoln Center. 'That's when I first really read it and listened to it,' he says. 'I laughed out loud. I liked it a lot. And I was also very aware of how it was perceived as either the greatest musical of all time or everyone's favourite musical, whether or not they'd seen it. But that was not intimidating enough to prevent me from saying, Okay, yeah, I want to do this. But before we really got it rolling, I read John Guare's *Six Degrees of Separation*, and I had to do that.'...

After five successful years and four successful shows at Lincoln Center Theater, Zaks left in 1990 because the works he wanted to select were subject to the approval of the artistic director, Gregory Mosher. When that approval was withheld on Barbara Lebow's play *A Shayna Maidel* and the Stephen Sondheim-John Weidman musical *Assassins*, Zaks realized it was not a condition he wanted to live with. Zaks directed *Assassins* at Playwrights' Horizons, and a Steve Tesich play called *Square One* at the Second Stage. Then he entered into an agreement with Rocco Landesman at Jujamcyn under which Zaks would be given a comfortable salary, office space, and support staff in exchange for a right of first refusal to house commercial productions of his work in the organization's five theatres. It was the kind of housekeeping deal that is popular in the film industry, but is unprecedented in New York commercial theatre; it represented an innovative and savvy wager by Landesman, whose affinity for gambling has served him well on Broadway. If rumours at the time were true, and Zaks was indeed interested in *Guys and Dolls*, that alone was enough to secure Jujamcyn's investment... His agent, Bill Craver, called and informed him that Lincoln Center's rights had expired, a number of commercial producers were competing for the rights, and whoever got them was going to offer the show to Zaks...

So Zaks committed to the material, but not to any of the competing producers. When the rights holders, Jo Loesser and Ann Burrows, selected Michael David and the Dodgers as their producers, Zaks signed on. Landesman was a founding member of the Dodgers and had worked regularly with them since joining Jujamcyn, which made it a perfect fit for Zaks.

Zaks began work on the show during the summer of 1991, six months before rehearsals were to commence.

'The first consideration for me was,' Zaks says, 'what was the set going to look like and how was it going to work? The solution was inspired by a visit I made to Tony Walton's home in Sag Harbor about six years ago. There he showed me a book of plays by Oscar Wilde - or it could have been Shaw - and Tony had done the illustrations. They were extraordinary. And I thought, wouldn't it be something if we did a show and that whole show was Tony's paintings, his palette! Wouldn't that impose an extraordinary design unity!

'As I studied the play, I knew it would have to be of a mythic size that takes the realism out of New York and leaves us with a romantic myth. The show is subtitled A Musical Fable of Broadway. It's not a cartoon, because cartoons suggest the unreal, the phony. It's a myth grounded in reality...

'I kept reading the play over and over and asking myself, was there any way to do this as a wraparound design? How are we going to be different? I called Cy Feuer, who produced the original, and asked if he had ever tried it with revolves, turntables. He said he did in L.A. and it didn't work. I couldn't come up with the answer.

'All the alternatives Tony or I thought of seemed to endanger the tempo that had to be maintained. The transitions would take too much time. Finally we came up with the right solution - to do it just the way they wrote it, just the way they did it, alternating between scenes in which the actors are very close to the audience, and then a stage full of energy and lots of people. So Tony and I committed to doing it that way, but not to hold back with the paintbrush, to use the boldest, brightest colours.'

With Walton working on preliminary sketches, Zaks then turned his attention to finding a choreographer.

'I didn't know who to go to,' Zaks says. 'This person would have to be as good at what they do, to put it bluntly, as I am at what I do. It had to be someone whose work made me feel that, if I were a choreographer, that's what I would have done. How do you find that out? I decided to have some choreographers do presentations for me.

'I felt a little guilty about this. It's a difficult question whether directors should be permitted to do this. But I found it to be an extraordinarily valuable tool for making a decision.'

Zaks admits he did not think much about the politics of such a presentation, which he regrets. Aside from those auditioning, he was putting dancers in the awkward position of having to accept the invitation to help out even if they did not want to, in fear of having the choreographers blackball them from show jobs if they refused to cooperate. Conversely, those who did cooperate would be expecting jobs if the choreographer got hired. It was another case of extreme awkwardness created by the fact that there is a whole generation of people who have not had the opportunity to demonstrate their work as previous generations had.

Zaks prefers not to discuss the six choreographers (some, including Jerry Mitchell, D.J. Giagni, Joey McNeeley, and Tony Stevens, accepted; others, including Wayne Cilento, declined) who were invited to make presentations and were not selected. The seventh, and the first to present, was Christopher Chadman, once a favourite dancer of Bob Fosse's, and Fosse's assistant on his last show, *Big Deal*. Most of Chadman's choreographic work had been done in regional theatres. But he wrote Zaks a letter and was invited to meet with him.

'I told him I wanted it to be Broadway dance,' Zaks says, 'athletic, vital, sexy - Jack Cole-Bob Fosse dancing. Some cross between jazz and modern with show biz thrown in. He said, That's what I do.'

Zaks asked Chadman and each of the others to get together a group of as many dancers as they needed and to stage three pieces: 'Runyonland,' the show's opening sequence, to demonstrate storytelling ability; 'Take Back Your Mink,' a nightclub number, to show how he would work with the girls; and the crapshooters' ballet, to demonstrate athletic dancing. The producers would cover expenses for the dancers and the space and give the choreographers a small stipend.

'Chadman's seven-and-a-half minute "Runyonland" was terrific, funny, lively,' Zaks says. 'In "Take Back Your Mink," the girls were very attractive, very sexy. I had some notes about it, but it was very good. But when his crapshooters' ballet was over I just went, "Wow!" It wasn't finished, but it was exciting. The best parts of it were there. And if it did that to me, I figured it would do it to the audience. In the bank...'

By the end of the summer, Zaks had his designer and his choreographer working. He asked costume designer William Ivey Long and lighting designer Paul Gallo, both of whom worked together with him and Walton often, to join the team. Additionally, Eddie Strauss came aboard; he had been the musical director of *Anything Goes* and did some planning on *Guys and Dolls* when Zaks was thinking of it for Lincoln Center. Zaks and Strauss invited orchestrator Michael Starobin, who had worked with them on *Assassins*, to listen to the score with them. Together they decided they wanted a bigger sound and quicker tempos in many places, so Starobin went to work re-orchestrating in a style that would fit with what was kept from George Bassman's and Ted Royal's work on the original production.

With his team in place and working, Zaks turned to casting. Zaks is labouring and meticulous in his casting efforts, and the process for this show went on for five months on two coasts. With a billboard of the show's logo hanging over Times Square by September and very little other musical theatre promised for the season, the press so eagerly anticipated who would be selected for the four famous lead roles that rumours-presented-as-fact kept showing up in gossip columns. This creates audience interest in the show. But it also results in having to put out a lot of fires with embarrassed phone calls to actors' agents to explain that their clients are not being offered jobs.

Rumours had Kevin Kline, Mandy Patinkin, and James Naughton offered Sky Masterson, Judith Ivey offered Adelaide, Bernadette Peters offered Adelaide and/or Sarah. Actually, all of these people were offered these roles - but not for this production. About five years earlier, producer Manny Azenberg had the rights, hired Michael Kidd, the original show's choreographer, to direct and choreograph this time out, and had conducted a lengthy and comprehensive search for well-known stars. Azenberg, the astute producer of most of Neil Simon's works, was well aware of the history of Broadway revivals without ticket-selling names above the title. Finally, Azenberg was ready to go with Ron Silver as Nathan Detroit, Patti Cohenour as Sarah, and Judith Ivey as Adelaide - as long as he could corral a star to play Sky. Azenberg thought he had one when Tom Selleck sang - and apparently sang well - for Michael Kidd. When Selleck's film career got in the way, however, the effort fell apart.

'When I began casting I was torn between wanting to do my own version and the fact that they got it right the first time,' Zaks says. 'How affected would I be by what they had done? How willing was I to go beyond that? And if I were to go beyond that, why? You've got to have a good reason to put actors on roller skates if they didn't do that originally. And Nicely-Nicely is the perfect example of what I'm talking about.'

Nicely-Nicely Johnson, a pal and messenger of floating-crap-game entrepreneur Nathan Detroit, who gets to sing the 11 o'clock showstopper 'Sit Down, You're Rockin' The Boat,' is a role that for over forty years has been associated with just one actor - Stubby Kaye. Kaye played it in the original show in 1950, he played it in the movie in 1955, he's been playing it in stock productions ever since. When Azenberg and company were planning their revival, only one name was discussed for the role - Stubby Kaye. Stubby Kaye has two distinguishing characteristics - he has a big, lovely tenor voice; and he is very fat.

'When I started to look for Nicely, I had an idea,' Zaks says. 'The idea was that he should be a big fat guy. Why shouldn't I do it that way? So in come all the big fat guys, but they don't turn me on. They weren't funny, they weren't lively, and they had inadequate voices. You need a big voice in that role, and a sense of joy, and must be larger than life. I saw a lot of gross overactors. And a lot of effeminate guys. They were all fat, but none of them was large, in the mythic sense. There are large actors, and then there are large actors.

'Nicely-Nicely Johnson is a role that for over forty years has been associated with just one actor - Stubby Kaye', seen here with fellow members of the cast of the 1953 London premiere.

'After a month, I was really desperate and I had Walter Bobbie come in. I had worked with him a number of times, and he had this big, strong kind of tenor voice that embraced you. It was a shot out of a gun and put a big grin on your face. But he's not big and fat. Walter projected skill and joy. So now I torment. I have him in a couple more times. I wonder if by casting him I'm abusing some essential something in the show that I'm not in touch with. I'm doing the show a disservice. I'm in tumult. I want to go with Walter. No, I'm not. I can't. Why can't I? I want a big fat guy to walk in the door and do exactly what Walter did. Then I remember, this is exactly

'Nathan Lane comes in and you know he's one of the funniest guys in the world.'
Nathan Lane (Nathan) and Peter Gallagher (Sky) in Jerry Zaks's 1992 Broadway revival.

what happened to him when they were casting the original Broadway company of *Grease*. He auditioned great but they wanted a big, heavy guy. Finally they went with him and he knocked them out. So I hired him.'

As is the case with almost every musical, casting began with contacting a lot of Hollywood stars who reportedly can sing. After the West Coast contingent has been run through, to no avail, comes the Broadway-musical A-list - people who want to do both movies and theatre, but if they do theatre they don't want to do a revival.

'I didn't like what I felt like, trying to entice someone to do the show,' Zaks says. 'Certainly the most serious mistakes I've made in my whole professional life have occurred when trying to convince anyone to do anything. Then the prevailing wisdom was actually articulated, that no revival had succeeded without stars. For me that's like hearing that no show ever worked on a Lincoln Center stage. That's a motivator. So I abandoned the idea of doing it with stars. It took the joy out of it for me, pursuing them and being rejected.'

In a phone conversation I had with Zaks early on in the casting process, the only thing he would say to me was, 'Nathan Lane's going to end up in there someplace.'

Zaks now says, 'Nathan Lane comes in, and you know he's one of the funniest guys in the world. And you think, Nathan's Nathan Detroit. Then you start talking yourself into and out of things. Maybe he's too young. He's supposed to be older. Maybe I should cast so-and-so because he's a little more Jewish. Then you hear fifty to a hundred people read Nathan Detroit, and Nathan Lane comes in again and you laugh so hard your stomach hurts. You gotta have him. Then he's done and you ask yourself, I laughed, but will an audience laugh? Am I laughing because I love Nathan Lane so much, or because he's good as Nathan Detroit? Does it matter? I'm laughing. And something extraordinary happened when he was in the room. So he's hired.

'I knew of Faith Prince though I didn't see her in *Jerome Robbins' Broadway*. A lot of people who auditioned for Adelaide had different things to recommend them. Then there were a lot who acted stupid, though Adelaide is smart. But for the total package, nobody came close to Faith. She knocked me out in her first audition and I wanted her. The funny voice, the funny look, but they were totally incidental to her reading of the lines. She was absolutely believable. And she had the voice to hit those notes at the end of "Lament" ["... bad, bad cold"]. If you can't rock the people with that note, you can't get it done.

'Sky Masterson was the only role for which there was a dead heat. Peter Gallagher came in and knocked me out. Again, he was a little on the young side. And Jimmy Naughton was a real consideration. I quickly discarded the idea that somehow his having done *City of Angels* so recently should be a reason why we shouldn't consider him. His presence onstage is strong and somehow reassuring. I feel very good when he's onstage. But it comes down to a feeling; the sound of one voice as opposed to another. I don't know how to explain it. I went with Peter.'

The most difficult of the four leads for Zaks to cast was the character of Sarah Brown. It would seem that if you made a list of working Broadway actors who were right for each of the four leads, the Sarah Brown list would be the longest. But Zaks told me before casting even began that he had an untraditional take on the role. He felt that the relationship between Sky and Sarah was the most difficult part of the show to make work. So he thought he might cast Sarah older than usual, have her be more of an experienced woman who had a lot of life and intelligence. 'I didn't want Sky to have to fall for a beautiful bimbo,' he says.

Then, when he was going to audition in Los Angeles, Zaks received a phone call from his friend Carolyn Mignini, with whom he had appeared on Broadway in *Tintypes*. Carolyn had been living out west with her husband, actor Steve Vinovich, and their two kids, and working in television for the past five years. Zaks said he was thinking of someone a little younger, but that Carolyn should read the show again and, if she wanted, come in and audition.

'She came in and sang "If I Were a Bell",' Zaks said. 'She's always been to my mind a good actress, and she is very witty and has character and a lovely voice. I found her audition thrilling. But I wondered, why? Did I just see an old friend give a great audition, or did I just find my Sarah Brown?' Zaks's decision came down to Josie de Guzman, Patty Ben-Petersen, and Carolyn. 'Ultimately, I decided Carolyn would work best for the relationship with Sky,' he says. 'At least, that's what I thought. Maybe I was casting with my heart.'…

Zaks felt he began rehearsals for *Guys and Dolls* with a sound battle plan. It had either grown out of the discussions with Tony Walton about the style of the scenery or subconsciously informed those talks. After agreeing with Walton that the designer would be aggressive in his use of bright colour, he encouraged William Ivey Long to be as uninhibited in designing the costumes. Now he needed a show that was big enough in performance to fill that space and those clothes. What Zaks was doing was getting away from the reality of New York City outside the theatre's doors and into a heightened, romantic version of the place. He would be attempting to make a large part of his audience re-imagine their hometown.

'To me, a successful show is like having a wonderful dream,' he says. 'Not a nightmare, but a wonderful dream where strangely improbable things happen, but you never question the logic of it in your dream. It always makes sense.

'I had to allow myself to believe,' he says, 'that on some level, because it was a great show, a classic musical, somehow I wouldn't have to work as hard to find the answers - that the answers were in there.'

But about three weeks into rehearsal, Zaks recalls, he found himself 'uncharacteristically discouraged and almost transparently depressed'.

'It was around the time that *Crazy for You* opened and received great reviews,' he says. 'And *The Most Happy Fella* had already opened to a good critical response. I was aware that the gosh-darn relationship between Sky and Sarah (Peter Gallagher and Carolyn Mignini) was not really happening. I was concerned that Walter (Bobbie) seemed self-conscious in rehearsals and maybe he was not as exciting a choice as I had felt during the audition.'

At a full run-through in the third week of rehearsals, Zaks's concerns were apparent. On the positive side, Faith Prince was already giving a memorable performance as Adelaide. The acting style of the show was very big, and Nathan Lane was bigger than everyone else, but very funny. The ensemble, particularly the collection of gamblers, was appealing and zany, and Chris Chadman's choreography took advantage of their personalities. The show was also filled with the kind of comic business that is one of Zaks's trademarks - such as Prince and Lane getting stuck together on a note during their counterpoint in 'Sue Me' and playing chicken to see who would quit first; and all the gamblers in the sewer popping up in the air when the very big Big Julie follows his toss of the dice with a Rumpelstiltskin-like jump.

But on the negative side, there was very little connection between Gallagher and Mignini. Her Sarah seemed too worldly, just too plain smart to fall for Sky Masterson's suave routine. Her performance was of a different size than the overall style of the show. And Bobbie had not found a style for Nicely and seemed to be self-consciously searching. He had the timidity that results from insecurity, which badly affected both the popular title tune and 'Sit Down, You're Rockin' The Boat.'

'I realized that I had somehow nudged Carolyn in the wrong direction,' Zaks says. 'It was a sterner and more businesslike approach to Sky and the

'Walter began to recapture the joy he had had doing auditions.' Walter Bobbie and cast rockin' the boat in Jerry Zaks's 1992 Broadway revival.

world than was right. We were trying to make the point that she was more tight-assed to begin with and that by virtue of getting to know him she lets her hair down. That is true to a certain extent in the dynamics of the way the relationship is written. But I pushed her so much the wrong way that you wondered, What could Sky possibly find appealing about her? So I pointed it out and both she and Peter worked very hard to make it work, and I wanted to believe that it was honestly on its way to working.

'Nicely was written for a fat guy, but it wasn't being performed by a fat guy. It kept me from being as happy about what Walter was doing as I wanted to be at the time. Walter could sense that and he was not happy with what he was doing, so he kept trying to force things. I didn't feel that what he was doing was of our world, but I couldn't put my finger on it. Maybe it was too big in a false kind of way.

'So Walter and I went through an extraordinary process of finding out who this character was. He kept trying to find the right size of performance. Sometimes it would be too much and he seemed brain-damaged, like Crazy Guggenheim. He would experiment in a way that was either self-serving or indulgent - and I wasn't very understanding. There was one scene where Nicely came on eating. It was the only indication that he had to be fat, but it was there. He would bring in an apple and a milkshake and a bag of groceries, keep trying to fix it with props. Then one night he came in and showed me this big carrot. And I laughed and said, No, no, no, I don't think so. But I miscommunicated and he didn't realize I really didn't want to see the carrot. When I saw the carrot, I got so mad, I said to myself, Okay, I'll cut the fucking scene. And I did. And now there was no reference to Nicely being fat. And the role started to work. He began to recapture the joy he had had during auditions - out of my anger.

'My impulse was frustration at how to make it work. The script was so sacred I never considered that it was an extraneous moment. But Walter's problems with the moment forced me to have to consider it. When things wouldn't work it would enrage me. Rage forced me to consider whether the scene was necessary, and it absolved Walter of having to do something that was not right for him.'…

Zaks began to get back his confidence in technical rehearsals at the Martin Beck Theatre during the week before previews began. All the design elements looked great and Chadman's dancing filled the theatre space and Zaks looked forward to getting an audience in.

On Monday night, 16 March *Guys and Dolls* played its first preview before a full house. Zaks stood in the back of the house and saw 'bad entrances, bad exits, bad scenes, a bad scene before "Sit Down, You're Rockin' The Boat" that hurt the number, slow pacing, self-indulgence, a lot of work that was not finished.

'People I knew came out of the theatre and avoided making eye contact with me,' Zaks says. 'I was not seeing any of the enthusiasm for something I've worked on that I usually see. And I realized, it's not special; we haven't made it special enough....

'I worked harder on this show than I've worked on anything in my life, particularly from the time we got into previews. That's when I did major surgery, because the audience told me they needed it - and they don't lie. Until then, it's all theoretical. It doesn't mean shit. Now you really go to work.'

There are five producers listed above the title in the *Playbill* for *Guys and Dolls*, four of which are producing organizations with a few principals. There are also two associate producers. The agreement between Zaks and Michael David, the lead producer, was that all producers would speak to David, and only he would relay their thoughts to Zaks. One of the unusual things about this production is that Zaks does not feel that agreement was ever violated.

David's first comment to Zaks was that the 'Runyonland' sequence, Chadman's seven-and-a-half-minute opening ballet, was falling flat. 'I had felt that before,' Zaks says. 'But hearing him say it, it automatically became something I had to deal with. I had hoped it would work better. You know these things stay in in proportion to how long you want to hope they will get better by themselves. They usually don't.

'The number was killing us, because you're asking the audience to follow a story in dance about characters we never see again, who are not important. When I told Chris Chadman we had to compress it, he said, No, let's throw it out and think of something else. It's not working. And that's why I can't wait to do another show with Chris.'

In the second week of the four-and-a-half-week preview period, 'Runyonland' was excised from the show. The evening now began with a bleed through a scrim to a stage filled with New Yorkers, ... then cleared for the first song, 'Fugue for Tinhorns.'

This was the most difficult period as Zaks studied his show to focus on the faults. 'I didn't know it at the time,' he says, 'but I think it took a full two weeks for the cast just to grow into the sets and costumes. It also takes at least a week or two for me to let go of things that I was convinced were working in the rehearsal hall. It's a tough two weeks to get through, but it's a critical part of the process.'...

One of the things that surprised Zaks most was how poorly the audience was responding to Nathan Lane's performance as Nathan Detroit. 'I was really enjoying him in rehearsals,' Zaks says, 'but when he got onstage, the audience didn't understand a thing he was saying for five minutes because he was so overwrought. They didn't get a chance to know him. It's the beginning of the play, things are going badly for the character, but you don't want to cut your throat yet! But Nathan's got great technique and understands what's happening. He needed to be encouraged to trust the material.

'He had this speech at the top, before Sky enters, and we laughed at it in the rehearsal hall. It was not funny. It was not funny to an audience. But we laughed because it was Nathan Lane and we all know him. We love him so we laughed because we didn't believe anyone could be so bold. But we didn't pay sixty bucks! Both Nathan and Faith Prince had played their roles before. They both had memories of that, which they let go of fairly easily, which is not always easy to do when you've gotten laughs. But I suspect that Nathan did that particular speech that way in the past and it worked, and now he was forced to try something else. He made the adjustment to take himself a little more seriously and not be quite as much on the verge of hysteria. Now the moment when he really did get angry paid off because we, the audience, had gotten to know him.'

Zaks made a lot of small adjustments within scenes - lines, entrances. positioning. 'It's all about making the storytelling better and better until you get it right,' he says.

He changed the first entrance of the Mission Band, which is the first time we get to meet Sarah Brown. Originally he filled the stage with people immediately following 'Fugue for Tinhorns,' then brought the band on through the crowd. But the band was getting lost. So Zaks reversed it, having the band come on immediately following the applause for the number, then having the rest of the people come on and gather around them.

Though Walter Bobbie had made great progress as Nicely, his numbers were still not landing as well as Zaks had hoped for. So the director quickened the tempo on the title song and gave Bobbie a high note to hold at the end of 'Sit Down, You're Rockin' The Boat.' Now the audience responded more enthusiastically.

'In the first scene between Sky and Sarah,' Zaks says, 'she says, "Mr Masterson, why are you here?'

'"I told you, I'm a sinner."

'"You're lying."

'His next line is, "Well, lying's a sin."

'There's only one way to say that line to be funny. And Peter wasn't saying it in that way. I listen to it over and over and then I get it. If it's anything but a simple throwaway, it doesn't pull the rug out from under Sarah and make us laugh. As much as the line is funny, it's her reaction that gets the laugh. You must say it in a way that will make her speechless.

'Then, at the end of "I've Never Been in Love Before," Sky and Sarah kiss and the Mission Band comes in and sees them. And Arvide [eventually cast with John Carpenter] says, "Good morning, Brother Masterson," and that gets sort of a chuckle. Now I'm home in the shower one night - why do these things always come in the shower? - and I go, He should hit the drum. He should hit the drum. What is he wearing the fucking thing around his neck for? Now we get two free laughs there. The applause ends, they're kissing, the band comes on and stands and stares at them. That's a laugh. Then Arvide hits the drum. Another laugh.

'Then there's the scene right before "Sit Down, You're Rockin' The Boat." Brannigan, a cop, comes in. Nathan puts his hat on his finger, says, "We will now hear from Brother Nicely Nicely Johnson."

'Walter starts to stand up very slowly and says, "It's like in a dream." Song.

'One night I say to Jill, Why the hell does he sing "Sit Down, You're Rockin' The Boat"?

'Then I'm in the shower again and it all comes to me. I see the whole scene. So I go in, call the company together, and say, Okay, there are two ways we can do it: this way, and I describe what we've been doing, or this way - Brannigan comes in and everybody screams. He's here to arrest you. Nathan jumps up and he's ad-libbing so you don't get arrested. Everyone ad-libs. Harry the Horse does his line. Then "We will now hear from Nicely"… Walter jumps up and acts harder than he ever has before. His dream's an ad-lib, the song's an ad-lib. Everyone's falling over themselves to keep from being arrested. Now it's funny.

'That simple adjustment made all the difference. It's all these little things. Looking for jokes. I love this stuff.'

Zaks did not expect to make any more changes in the top of the show once the original 'Runyonland' was cut. But about two weeks before opening night, Chadman came to him and said, 'I got something else. I'll need everyone in the rehearsal hall at in the morning.'

The cast arrived at 11am and Chadman taught his new one-and-a-half-minute version of 'Runyonland.' Zaks came in at two o'clock to have a look and said, 'That's it.'

But with all the fixes, something was still gnawing away at Zaks - there was no romantic spark between Sky and Sarah. The audience did not find it credible that Sky would be knocked out by who she was. And since the whole last twenty minutes of the first act is about their relationship, if this didn't work, the audience would spend the intermission disappointed. Zaks resisted giving up on its working. He knew that, based on a one-year contract for the show, Mignini had rented out her house in Los Angeles, moved her family to New York, and put her kids in school there. But there was grumbling among the producers.

'Finally, having done as much as I could, I tried to look at the show as objectively as I could,' Zaks says, 'as if I had paid sixty bucks and was totally unaware of any of the personalities involved. And it was not right.'

With eight days remaining until the critics were to see the show, Zaks felt that if he did not make the change now, there would not be enough time to prepare another actress to fill the role by opening night. He called Mignini at home first thing in the morning and told her that Josie de Guzman, her understudy, would be going on that night.

'I don't know how much of it was my responsibility and how much of it is just who Carolyn is chemically,' Zaks says, 'and how much of it was triggered by my own anxiety that it wasn't working, which I'm sure she picked up on.'

De Guzman, who had herself been fired earlier in the season from *Nick & Nora*, was told she was a temporary replacement. But Zaks liked what he saw from the get-go.

'Finally, it was about five days before the critics came,' Zaks says, 'and I stood in the back of the house watching and I went, This is good now. I stood there *kvelling* rather than wanting to kill. I don't know how to tell you. The rage I experience when it's not right is really considerable. The joy that I feel when it is right is great.'

A golf bag leaned against the wall in Jerry Zaks's office. He eyed it like Adelaide eyeing a wedding veil. It was two and a half weeks since *Guys and Dolls* opened officially, and the show appeared to have the makings of a theatre phenomenon. The day the critics' notices ran, the show set the one-day record for a daily box-office take, surpassing *The Phantom of the Opera*. That long-absent Broadway prize - a line at the ticket window - was a constant outside the Martin Beck Theatre. The show was about to have cover stories in New York and Newsweek magazines, and Faith Prince was getting the kind of star treatment from the media that hadn't been seen in town since Michael Crawford had opened as the Phantom.

'Why has there been such a response?' Zaks says. 'I'm the wrong guy to explain it. On the one hand I want to say, So why not? If it's in proportion to how relentlessly we tried to make this universally recognised wonderful show as wonderful as people think they remember it, or as wonderful as it is on paper, then it seems to be just.

'But of course it's not that. I don't know how to explain it sociologically or historically or temperamentally. I don't know how it relates to the current work in New York or to people's need for a wonderful fairy tale or fable. I want to believe it's connected to people just wanting to see a really first-rate production of really first-rate material on Broadway. Words and relationships. Something spiritually uplifting - the way that synagogue was when people were standing and singing together. For me that was like, Wow! Electricity. We're talking about impulses and emotions and not anything cerebral. Electricity is not intellectual. But when it happens to the audience or the critics, they rush out and tell everyone else.

'Laughter is not the function of a cerebral reaction. It has to do with the natural human need for joy in life. Like the sunflower turns to the sun. We want to laugh. We want to experience it.'

GUYS AND DOLLS

a musical fable of Broadway
Based on a story and characters of **Damon Runyon**
Music and Lyrics by **Frank Loesser**
Book by **Jo Swerling & Abe Burrows**

Opening: **The Olivier Theatre** 17 December 1996
The production was first seen in the Olivier on 9 March 1982

Characters, in order of appearance

Benny Southstreet	**Wayne Cater**
Nicely-Nicely Johnson	**Clive Rowe**
Rusty Charley	**Connor Byrne**
Sarah Brown	**Joanna Riding**
Arvide Abernathy	**John Normington**
The Mission Band	
Agatha	**Freya Copeland**
Calvin	**Kevin Walton**
Martha	**Katy Secombe**
Harry the Horse	**Steven Speirs**
Lieutenant Brannigan	**Colin Stinton**
Nathan Detroit	**Henry Goodman**
The Crapshooters	
Angie the Ox	**Tom Hodgkins**
Brandy Bottle Bates	**Kevin Rooney**
Scranton Slim	**Kieran Creggan**
Joe the Joker	**Christopher Beck**
Regret	**Kevin Walton**
Society Max	**Kraig Thornber**
Benny the Greek	**Anthony Renshaw**
Hot-Horse Herbie	**John Tobias**
Sky Rocket	**James Davies**
Miss Adelaide	**Imelda Staunton**
Hot Box Girls	**Jane Fowler**
	Suzanne Maria Thomas
Sky Masterson	**Clarke Peters**
Voice of Joey Biltmore	**Tom Hodgkins**
Master of Ceremonies	**Kraig Thornber**

More Hot Box Girls	**Freya Copeland**
	Katy Secombe
Mimi	**Rae Baker**
General Matilda B Cartwright	**Sharon D Clarke**
Big Jule	**Stanley Townsend**
Drunk	**Anthony Renshaw**
Waiter in the Hot Box	**Christopher Beck**
Ensemble/Swing	**Philip Campbell**
Swing	**Janine Davies**

Director	**Richard Eyre**
Musical Staging	**David Toguri**
Settings	**John Gunter**
Costumes	**Sue Blane**
Lighting	**David Hersey**
Music Director	**Tony Britten**
Associate Music Director	**Mark W Dorrell**
Orchestrations	**Tony Britten & Terry Davies**
Assistant Music Director	**Steven Edis**
Dialect Coach	**Joan Washington**
Company Voice Work	**Patsy Rodenburg**
Sound	**Paul Groothuis**
Assistant Choreographer	**Cristina Avery**
Production Photographer	**John Haynes**

The Choo-Choo Band

Conductor/keyboard	**Mark W Dorrell/Tony Britten**
Piano/assistant conductor	**Steven Edis**
Flute/piccolo/alto sax	**Ray Warleigh**
Clarinet/soprano & tenor sax	**Timothy Holmes**
Flute/clarinet/tenor sax	**David Roach**
Flute/bass clarinet/baritone sax	**Emma Fowler**
Trumpet	**Martin Drover**
Trumpet	**Graham Russell**
Tenor trombone	**Paul Nieman**
Bass trombone	**Andy Fawbert**
Guitar/banjo	**Mitch Dalton**
Double bass/bass guitar	**Lennie Bush**
Drums	**Ian Green**
Percussion	**Nicholas Ormrod**

LONDON 1996

Matt Wolf

The theatre is an ephemeral art, which makes it a medium at once thrilling and sad. Witness a particularly moving performance, and you leave on a high, wondering whether the show could ever be as good again. But try to recapture that performance years later, and all that remains are memories (and the occasional grainy archival video). Unlike a film, which endures, in the theatre one generally can't recapture the original – unless you're Carol Channing, forever reprising *Hello, Dolly!*

In a league apart are the creators of the National Theatre's 1982 production of *Guys and Dolls*, who are playing considerable odds in attempting to make history twice. When the production first opened, they had everything to prove; having proven it resoundingly, they might now be seen to have more to lose, or at the very least to be playing safe. But in the way of film directors whose sequels surpass their originals – Francis Coppola's *The Godfather, Part II*, for instance – a revival of a revival need not be a rehash. 'This will not be *le pot réchauffé*,' Richard Eyre said late in '95, discussing his idea of revisiting a beloved classic. What remained was to see how this musical might be delivered up afresh. Herewith, some snapshots from a show in progress, alongside a look at the players – on and off stage – hoping to make *Guys and Dolls* sing.

THURSDAY, 31 OCTOBER

It is nearing the end of the second week of rehearsal, and 26 of the 28-strong company are gathered in the Royal National Theatre's Rehearsal Room One on the ground floor for their morning warm-up. At a table sits David Toguri, the Vancouver-born choreographer of Japanese parentage responsible nearly 15 years ago for making a physical whole out of a company who, Julia McKenzie excepted, were not exactly top-heavy in tap expertise.

In the intervening period, musicals have proliferated in Britain. As a result, more can be expected from performers in them, especially since four of this company are proper show dancers. As for the rest, Toguri says, 'Actors are better trained now at drama school; they take movement and singing. They're not as green as the first group.' At the moment, Toguri is 'still finding out what they can do,' but he remains heartened by the presence of one figure in the back row gamely shuffling and tapping away as he did before – Richard Eyre.

The principals this time have far more extensive musical credentials: several of them, indeed, are products of the National's own *de facto* school of musicals. Playing Nicely-Nicely Johnson is Clive Rowe, 32, a Guildhall graduate who won acclaim as the first-ever professional black Mr. Snow in Nicholas Hytner's 1992 production for the National of *Carousel*. Sister Sarah is Joanna Riding, 29, an alumna both of *Carousel* and the National's subsequent *A Little Night Music*, the Olivier auditorium's previous musical tenant.

John Normington and Joanna Riding

Imelda Staunton, Jane Fowler and Katy Secombe

A natural Nathan Detroit – though, surprisingly, a newcomer to the part – is Henry Goodman, 46, a self-described 'East End yob' who won an Olivier Award for Stephen Sondheim's *Assassins* and has made a specialty of the American canon in Arthur Miller's *Broken Glass*, Tony Kushner's *Angels in America* and the Cy Coleman musical *City of Angels*. 'There's no question, if I'm really honest, that I thought I'd have a break from American parts for a while and go back to what I am by birth and breeding and training – an English actor.' Offered the part in July, he went through 'much gnashing of teeth as to whether I should do it,' and says the 10 days' rehearsals to date have meant 'learning an enormous amount very quickly; we're working at a hell of a rate.'

What persuaded him to accept the part is the same fact that justifies the work: 'This musical is such fun.'

Veterans of the original production include John Normington's Arvide Abernathy, Sister Sarah's voice of solace and hope, who gets the musical's most quietly piercing number, 'More I Cannot Wish You.' Sky Masterson, Sarah's love interest, is Clarke Peters, the London-based American who took over the same role in the West End in 1985 having first played it as a 24-year-old in Watford – Peters' British debut – in 1976.

Former Hot Box girl Imelda Staunton was promoted to Miss Adelaide during the original run, and resumes that part now, having won a Best Musical Olivier Award in the interim for Stephen Sondheim's *Into the Woods*. 'I don't like musicals much but I've been lucky enough to do very special ones,' she says, explaining her return. 'I know how joyous this show is to be in, and it's not often you get an opportunity to do something you've loved so much twice.' Besides, as she points out, 'I was 26 then; now I'm 40. I'm much better casting now.'

Upstairs in Rehearsal Room Four, specific numbers are being worked up. Seated in a circle are Staunton and her Hot Box colleagues, squawking their way endearingly through 'Take Back Your Mink' attended to by Eyre, wearing a T-shirt commemorating the previous month's Broadway opening of his production of *Skylight*. At the piano is musical director Tony Britten, another 1982 veteran. Strains of Riding practising 'I'll Know' can be heard through the wall.

'Make it as bright and as high as you can 'eek it,' says Britten, referring to the unique vocal demands of the number. 'Don't be afraid to be nasal,' urges Eyre. 'You've got to really live out the horror of this – that the worst thing you could imagine is going to bed with a millionaire.' The song

Clive Rowe

'Sit Down, You're Rockin' The Boat'

is a cockeyed hymn to feminine independence, boasting among the oddest musical conjunction of words ever in the phrase 'to from whence it came.'

Eyre tells Staunton her elision of one phrase 'could be a little less tasteful.' She, in turn, does a quick Lina Lamont from *Singin' In The Rain*, adding later that she understands whence Adelaide came: 'I've sung to people who couldn't care less. I sang in a restaurant with people eating, and it was kind of demoralizing. You think, couldn't they just look at you?'

Britten, finishing the session, is in a complimentary mood: 'Very, very good, ladies. Well-squeaked.'

Clive Rowe is preparing an early rehearsal of 'Sit Down, You're Rockin' The Boat,' a number that can be counted upon to lift a giddy musical to heights of delirium. In the '82 production, American actor David Healy won an Olivier Award in the part, and got as many as five encores for relating to his fellow gamblers his dreamlike moment of salvation. Healy's death in October 1995, at 64, is one of four that haunts this production for those who were part of it originally. (Among them, the National's first Sky, Ian Charleson, who died of AIDS in January 1990.) 'There were quite a few tears at the readthrough,' says Joan Washington, then – as now – the production's dialect coach. The losses, she says, 'bring you up like a jolt.' 'The first day it was weird,' agrees John Normington. 'I looked around the room and there were so many ghosts.'

As it happens, Rowe has played Nicely before, at the Belgrade Theatre, Coventry, in 1987, fresh out of drama school. The National, though, is something else. 'I never thought I'd be playing the part again, especially not somewhere like this. The work process here is so involved that for me Nicely is a completely different character, a completely different person.'

How has Rowe's view of Nicely evolved? 'He's very young in his attitudes, in a way very innocent, even though he's a gambler. He's a complicated man: there's only one drive in his life, and that is food. He thinks, "If ever I was going to be anybody else, I would come back as Nathan Detroit." He tries to base himself on Nathan but fails miserably.'

'Sit Down' allows ample room for freedom of interpretation. The question is how far to go, especially since Rowe will be leading a hot gospel encore with Sharon D. Clarke, the Tottenham native cast as General Cartwright and a vivid scat-singer herself. Tony Britten offers Rowe general counsel: 'This is without a doubt the 11 o'clock spot; in that respect, it has a slightly out-of-context thing to it. It is a real rabble-rouser, but it is also a story, and it's important to remember that is what Nicely is getting off on,

John Gunter's neon Times Square

not the performance of it.'

Rowe has his own analysis. 'The challenge is to sit back on it, not to get carried away with the actual musicality and not to get to the end of it before you start. You have to take on board the situation – that the police are there and that this is a bible meeting; you have to think, this isn't the 11 o'clock number, but by the end have everyone jumping around.'

As he sings, his sweet tenor voice broadens into an enveloping and infectious glimpse of salvation; rarely has a gambler looked so cherubic. 'Brava, bellissima,' says Britten, acknowledging that now is the time to plan for encores – although, says Britten with the grin of someone confident he will be proven wrong, 'you probably won't get one.'

FRIDAY, 8 NOVEMBER

In 1982, *Guys and Dolls* was viewed in some quarters as the biggest risk the National Theatre had ever taken. Fail with a Shakespeare, and you knew other directors would be on hand to try other Shakespeare plays. But screw up the NT's first-ever musical, and you were sealing the fate – at least as far as that building was concerned – of a genre.

'It was a bold entrepreneurial gesture, you could say a foolish entrepreneurial gesture,' Richard Eyre is recalling in his corner office, looking out at the view he will leave behind in September 1997, when he hands over the artistic directorship to Trevor Nunn. In 1981, Eyre's predecessor, Peter Hall, invited Eyre to step in where Olivier had failed to go – in welcoming into the British subsidised theatre the one area, the musical, at which New York had long been deemed the master.

'When the critics said I'd written a love letter to Broadway, it was sort of half-true,' says Eyre. 'Actually I'm not a particular lover of musicals; what I'm in love with is American culture. Like all my generation, I was completely colonised, willingly colonised, by American culture. I'm a colonial product, like the sort of Indian that has grown up in India under the British empire and talks about Thomas Hardy.'

His idea was a *Guys and Dolls* steeped in Marvel comics and *Bilko* and yet wedded to the finest acting traditions of the English theatre. 'I had an idea that, however I did it, one had to apply the criteria one would apply to any other piece of work at the National Theatre; it had to be true to its genre but in a sense true to whatever the values were embodied within the NT.' In the ensemble scenes, the desired result was, in Eyre's view, 'a form of

Imelda Staunton and Henry Goodman with, left to right, John Tobias,
Kieran Creggan, Anthony Renshaw, Tom Hodgkins, Connor Byrne,
Steven Speirs and Colin Stinton

expressionism where people are taking a natural attitude and pushing it to its comic limit – a comic strip limit.' But on an individual basis, 'it had to be very well acted, at the very least, but of course being a musical, it had to be very well sung; otherwise I could just hypothesize about what people would say.'

Since then, Eyre has done only one other musical, the disappointing West End staging of *High Society*, despite being offered several, he says, 'that are still running' across the Thames. The National, meanwhile, established an exemplary track record in musicals, many by Stephen Sondheim, and one of them – Rodgers and Hammerstein's *Carousel* – so highly esteemed that it actually travelled on to New York, a formerly unthinkable case of musical theatre coals to Newcastle. (Eyre, by contrast, calls the idea of taking his *Guys and Dolls* to Broadway – either then or now – 'a folly too far; you'd be on a hiding to nothing.')

But why try *Guys and Dolls* again? The answer has less to do with the anticipated reason – Eyre's desire for closure within his own career as he prepares to move on – and more to do with the economic exigencies of running three auditoria year-round. Think practicality first, sentiment a distant second.

'It's pure financial logic,' says Eyre. 'We've got a problem filling a rather intractable 1200-seat theatre [the Olivier] 52 weeks of the year. The theatre is wholly uncongenial to an awful lot of drama. Any introspective drama simply doesn't work; what works are plays which acknowledge the existence of an audience, which have a public dimension.'

Continues Eyre: 'Unless you package the repertoire, it's not a theatre where you can take big risks. If you do the two *Oedipus* plays, you have to ensure you're in some way ballasting your box office prospects. You actually have to have your Christmas show; it's an unavoidable fact of theatre ecology.' (*Guys and Dolls* follows into the Olivier an autumn repertoire of Peter Hall's *Oedipus* productions and Ben Jonson's *The Alchemist*, directed by Bill Alexander.)

For some time Eyre had been considering Rodgers and Hart's *Pal Joey*, another musical from the golden age that produced *Guys and Dolls*. Unlike *Guys and Dolls*, the book on *Pal Joey* needs attention, and Eyre had even asked Tom Stoppard to revise the libretto, with Diana Rigg in mind for the starring role. But the fact is, says the director, '*Pal Joey* was a huge amount of work, and I simply didn't have either the appetite or the time to get *Pal Joey* in shape.' What was needed was something along the lines of a guaranteed Olivier hit, as *The Wind in the Willows* had been for four years or Boucicault's *The Shaughraun* for two.

'Rather shamefacedly,' Eyre recalls, he suggested *Guys and Dolls* at a staff meeting. 'I said, look, what are we going to do? Would it be crazy and shameful to revive *Guys and Dolls*, and everyone said wow, why don't you do that?, and I said, are you sure? But the last thing on my mind, and the thing I was embarrassed about, was that it would be seen as a self-indulgent valedictory gesture. It has absolutely nothing to do with that.'

Downstairs, the company is half way through the rehearsal period – three weeks finished, and three to go. Today, with Act Two Scene Five to work on – the run-up to, and including, 'Sit Down, You're Rockin' The Boat' – the consensus is that there is work to be done.

'We were screaming this morning,' says David Toguri, whose would-be dancers are not yet in sync. 'Visually, they've got to be absolutely together : one person out of step, and the number is killed.'

'I'm going to learn these lines one day,' says Steven Speirs, who is playing Harry the Horse. Speirs is from Troedyrhiw in Wales, which is some distance from the 'Noo Yawk' of *Guys and Dolls*. 'It's a long commute,' he admits, 'but I live in Greenwich.'

Then there's Joanna Riding's cornet. As a member of the Save-a-Soul Mission, the Lancashire-born farmer's daughter must toot her own horn in numbers like 'Follow the Fold,' where Sky Masterson spots the doll he will later whisk to Havana. 'I play two notes,' Riding smiles. 'A little bit of work is in order.' Not to mention 'getting fit enough to do all the running around while singing. We're doing circuits, aerobics, and tap; we all have very sore bottoms.'

25-year-old Wayne Cater, from Ammanford in South Wales, is grappling with the accent. As Benny Southstreet, he must deliver the Runyon-esque honk. 'New York is totally opposed to the Welsh accent. We slide into words, whereas New York comes straight in and drives straight through. I'm going, Jesus Christ, trying to keep the energy driving on, which isn't natural for a Welshman.' Still, he is thrilled to be in a production he saw when he was 11: 'I thought to myself, I must do this; now I am.'

The accents are the terrain of Joan Washington, who, since 1982, has become a leading dialect coach on both sides of the Atlantic : Barbra Streisand in *Yentl*, William Hurt in *Jane Eyre*, and Glenn Close in *101 Dalmatians* have numbered among her celebrity charges.

Imelda Staunton: 'Adelaide's Lament'

Runyon-speak, she says, has 'incredibly difficult rhythms. The basic premise of standard English is that it tends to stress at fairly equal intervals of time; what we need is for them to stress a line over a phrase rather than the individual words. *Guys and Dolls* is punctuated very specifically, but English actors love to add little commas, putting things in parentheses to break it up. The important thing is that the dialogue absolutely carry you forward, though sometimes the Runyonesque thing is about spelling it out, like it's written in neon.'

Guys and Dolls presents a motley set of challenges. In this version, Sky is from Colorado, so he has to sound vaguely western and very specifically the outsider – a task Peters, as an American, meets with ease. With Riding's Sister Sarah, says Washington, 'I want a very standard eastern seaboard sound so you don't really hear an accent; you just hopefully hear American.'

Miss Adelaide, by contrast, 'is an accent unto herself, but I don't think she should be alone in terms of what she does. She's got her famous song [Adelaide's Lament] with all its 'toins,' 'poissuns,' and 'goils'. But that sound should be coming right through all the guys; it's not just Miss Adelaide.' Elsewhere, the tasks are very specific: make sure Harry the Horse stresses the last syllable of 'cabaret,' while Big Jule hits the first of 'record.'

Accents have improved, Washington feels, since 1982. 'It used to be that everybody was not really caring and not quite committing to it. But young actors now are a quintessential TV/movie generation. They are brought up with no inhibitions about American accents; they do them all the time.'

Isn't there a risk that this show – any show – become over-accented, so that its sound becomes its subject? Washington agrees. 'It's not about being clever with an accent or trying to get a gag out of an accent, because in real terms, nobody's aware of the way they speak; nobody's aware they have an accent. My ultimate aim is that nobody notices, that the accents just get at the roots of the people.'

'Gamblers, gamblers,' barks Richard Eyre in his own best Runyon tones, calling the room to order, while Joanna Riding practises walking primly in high heels, later doing a little shuffle for good measure.

In the scene, General Cartwright is fretting over the non-arrival of followers at a Mission set to close, when Sky emerges providentially, bearing 'a dozen or so assorted sinners.' This afternoon's job is to take the scene out of chaos, as Sky's charges show up confused and guilty and scrambling for a seat ('titanic figures at the front,' calls out Eyre), and on

Clive Rowe, Henry Goodman, Anthony Renshaw and Wayne Cater

Clarke Peters and Joanna Riding

towards joy and the barely controlled euphoria of 'Sit Down, You're Rockin' The Boat.'

Wearing rehearsal jackets and hats, the men are in the process of individualising Runyon's low-lifers, their betting moves coached by David Gant, a London croupier. Suppressing his natural Dublin accent, Stanley Townsend's Big Jule – the most imposing tough guy East Cicero, Illinois ever produced – emits a basso profundo 'what's the pitch' that seems to surprise even himself. 'Conducting' the sinners – 'do it with a small baton,' says Eyre, reining in the actor's natural exuberance – is Henry Goodman, whose Nathan looks dapper, even courtly, in a red jacket. Not too courtly, though, to resist hoisting up Cater's short, squat Benny Southstreet to launch the confessions. 'I always was a bad guy and a gambler, but I ain't going to do it no more. I thank you,' says Cater on cue, sounding both breathless and morose.

Later, Eyre guides Clarke Peters and Joanna Riding through their first scene together that climaxes in a kiss – and in Sarah slapping Sky's cheek. 'Is that sexist or what?' asks Eyre, as he suggests an even smoother way of playing it. 'Is Sky sexist?' says Peters, looking surprised. Replies Eyre: 'I was talking about the director.'

WEDNESDAY, 20 NOVEMBER

Ten days before technical rehearsals, and Imelda Staunton has something to say as she walks by : 'We've made no progress since you were last here, and I refuse to do that nasty American accent.' 'We ain't got that much time left; that's the feeling at the moment,' says Irishman Connor Byrne, the Limerick native cast as Rusty Charley, who pauses to adjust his kneepads. 'Without them, you're dead.'

Rushing about is assistant stage manager Emma B. Lloyd, who is noting the necessary props. Lloyd joined the first production in the summer of '82, four months into its run.

'This is a medium show prop-wise,' says Lloyd, but a demanding one 'because the scenes are so short.' The gangsters, too, require lots of personal props – money, dice, combs, as well as bubble gum, lighters, personal notebooks. While performers await various items, Tom Hodgkins as Angie the Ox ('there's a lot of padding to come,' he says, looking only marginally ox-like) is mourning the loss of his hair. 'It's in a bag back home,' says Hodgkins, born in Australia to American parents but based in Britain since 1974. 'My wife is four-and-a-half years older than me and looks far better than I do.'

Richard Eyre, meanwhile, has strained a ligament in his right knee during those aerobic morning warm-ups – 'I'm off alcohol, which is disappointing,' he says, accepting an ice pack from an in-house nurse – but remains riveted on rehearsals, his halting gait notwithstanding. 'I'm in meetings every morning, and I find myself thinking, How soon can I slip away? The fact is, you would *pay* to do this.'

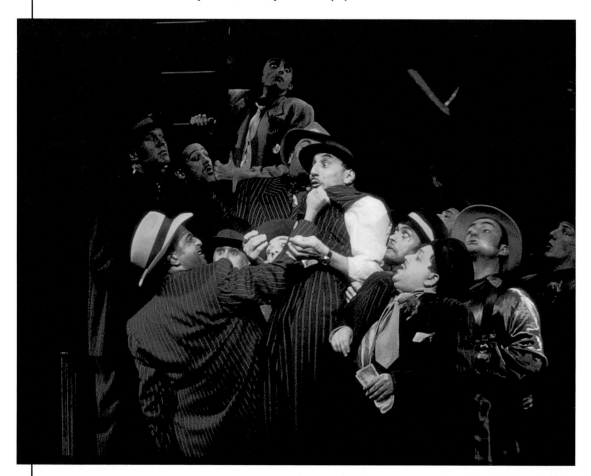

Henry Goodman in the grip of Stanley Townsend

Surveying his company, he finds them 'more homogeneous. Now guys in their 20s and 30s expect to sing and dance. They're more ambitious, so we've made some of the dancing [the closing tap routine, for example] more ambitious.'

Today's task includes working through the 'Sit Down, You're Rockin' The Boat' encores. (Deadpans Eyre: 'That's how cynical we are.') In front of him, the male chorus are carousing, waiting to be put through their paces. 'It's mayhem,' grins Clarke Peters. 'This company is like a bunch of naughty schoolboys – which is exactly what they've got to be.'

Peters is at rehearsals fresh from a reflexology session and shiatsu massage, and looks exceedingly mellow as he watches Toguri's complex moves, uttering the occasional 'Wow.' This is Peters' third stint playing Sky, and the character has changed as he has; different colleagues have had an effect, too.

In his 20s at Watford opposite Elizabeth Mansfield's Sarah, Peters saw Sky as 'a guy looking to pull the birds.' In the West End in 1985, he says, 'I thought wanting to cool out might be in the back of his mind after however many years on the road.' This time, he says, 'the intentions haven't

Clarke Peters: 'Luck, Be a Lady'

changed, but the moments that clarify the intentions have.' For that he credits his colleagues. 'With Jo, this brilliant energy comes out of her eyes. We're locking eye-to-eye contact. We're not just throwing words around; we're listening.'

Of Henry Goodman, Peters says this is 'the first time I've had a Nathan so frenetic, which allows me to be still. With Norman Rossington [in the West End] you felt you were trying to pull things out of him. Now, Sky can be a lot more centred.'

In 1985, newspapers were quick to make a point of the West End casting – 'Sky turns black,' read a typical headline – just as seven years later they raised a fuss about the casting of Clive Rowe as Mr. Snow in the National's *Carousel*. Four years on, both men hope their performances will be the topic of discussion, not the colour of their skin. 'If you can't have multi-racial casting, then how can you have what is in a sense multi-racial casting in life?' says Rowe, whose other credits include the Sam Mendes revival of *Company*, the first-ever Sondheim production to have – in Adrian Lester – a black male lead. 'The point is, you're a black actor, you're good in the part, and after that there's nothing to be said.'

Peters, though, acknowledges that comparable integrated casting is less easily tolerated in his home country. 'For Americans it becomes a power struggle. There are people who wouldn't want to see a black man in that particular role because he is the kingpin for the love interest. I know people get upset when they see a black man kissing a white woman on stage, but that is their problem. This show is not about black and white; it's not a racial issue. It's about men's hearts – their relationship with women – and that's the bottom line.'

Wayne Cater and Clive Rowe rehearse the title song, Loesser's paean to the feminine grip that, when it comes to men, exceeds even the power of dice. The two make an extraordinary pair: Cater as squarely solid as Rowe is fleshy, and yet both of them irresistibly open-faced and eager – Tweedledum and Tweedledee blessed by Terpsichore.

'Good boys, bloody hell,' Imelda Staunton exclaims admiringly when the number ends. Later, she describes the show as 'the most wonderful piece of tapestry, where you're given all these incredible silks and not one of us wants to put a stitch wrong. Everyone is aware of how perfect it is as a piece of work and knows it has to be beautifully made.' The first time around, 'we were terrified,' and yet she recalls an opening night that was "like being a

Clive Rowe and Wayne Cater

rock star. These guys won't believe the response they'll get; they'll be doing the encores twelve times.'

At other musicals, Staunton says, 'I see audiences standing, and I think, 'No, it's not good enough.' With us, no one stood and yet the applause was thick with gratitude; it was like the response to a fantastic play. Whether audiences have loosened up since, we'll see.' The actress met her husband – Jim Carter, who was playing Big Jule – in the original production, though he has decided to sit out this revival: 'We've got a three-year-old child, and we didn't think the two of us should be out every night for four months. But he envies me the joy of it.'

The production, she feels, had an impact beyond the NT run itself. 'Doing *Guys and Dolls* here moved musicals on in London. It absolutely gave people the courage to say, right then, let's try another damned American accent and go for it." People suddenly realised, she says, "that we've got fantastic actors, and that is what this is, an actor's musical. If you go to see a dancing show and they dance, you think, that's great. Here, you've got all these great character actors and suddenly they dance – it lifts your heart.'

How is Staunton holding up? 'OK OK,' she groans in mock-agony. And then: 'There aren't many better feelings.'

Clive Rowe, on his way out, admits to being "absolutely shattered. The only positiveness is that if I can get through that number ['Sit Down'] four times, I should be able to fly doing it once." He pauses. "It's been a huge afternoon."

THURSDAY, 21 NOVEMBER

3pm, time for the first run-through, and everyone is in attendance. Designer John Gunter – who has worked frequently with Eyre, both before and after the '82 productions – sits, notepad at the ready, joined for much of the afternoon by costume designer Sue Blane. (David Hersey is the lighting designer.) The look of the show was among the most remarked-upon aspects of the Olivier original: a seedy yet vibrant kaleidoscope of neon and colour that suggested Times Square refracted through a time warp, its influences as varied as Andreas Feininger's '40s photographs and Martin Scorsese's 1977 film, *New York , New York*.

In 1982, Gunter had not yet done a musical, though jobs since then have included the historic Trevor Nunn *Porgy and Bess* at Glyndebourne and an Australian touring production of *West Side Story*, directed by Ian Judge. As a 15-year-old he saw the London premiere of *Guys and Dolls* at the Coliseum in 1953 and went on to achieve a domestic reminder of the piece by marrying a New Yorker.

Looking back on his conception, Gunter says the aim was for a fairly realistic palette in keeping with the quality in Runyon, for all its buoyant cartoonishness, of something 'wonderfully, grubbily earthbound. Of course one can exaggerate the people or the personalities, but there's a reality in those characters that is worth exploring without it being too limiting.'

Explaining the colour scheme of a staging actually set in 1948 – 'I wanted that flavour of the post-War period,' Richard Eyre confirms – Gunter opted for a 'slightly monotone' beginning evocative of the films of the era giving way to neon that 'suddenly lights up and produces a completely different atmosphere – rather like the Vegas of old, when neon grew above it and transformed it into another society.' This set pre-dates the use of the famous – some would say infamous – Olivier drum revolve, which allowed other worlds to rise up from beneath the stage in productions like *The Wind in the Willows*. 'This was a push-and-pull show, which is even more surprising,' says Gunter. In our present age of hydraulics, it remains 'very under-mechanized.'

Sue Blane talks of costumes conveying 'that wonderful, gutsy old New York feel. There are sharp colours but they shouldn't be garish in a music-hall way, or garish for the sake of it.' With the men, the task was 'making people look like gangsters and sharks and gamblers. They get to look muscly and tough, with those wonderful pads that go right the way round, not just lifting the shoulder and sticking it out beyond the arm.'

The women are either Hot Box girls or Salvation Army employees. Accordingly, they wear boned leotards, like a swimsuit – 'it acts as both a costume and a corset,' says Blane – or straight uniforms for Sarah and her cohorts that should look pure without seeming naive.

Both artists have had to remake almost all their original designs from scratch. Blane has given what clothes remain from '82 to the actors to use during rehearsals: 'Only ghastly tatty bits are left; you couldn't wear them in performance.' Nothing remains from the first set except several tubes of neon, and they, says Gunter, got pressed into service in the film *Judge Dredd*.

Today's run represents Tony Britten's first opportunity to lead the company all the way through the show. Assistant music director Steven Edis – 'he is my rock,' says Britten – is on piano and will be joined in production by an orchestra totalling 13. That is about half the size of the Broadway version, a (mostly) economically determined fact that ultimately won the approval of the watchful Loesser estate.

The goal, says Britten, who co-orchestrated the revival with Terry Davies, was 'a hard-swinging Big Band sound' with a distinctly jazz feel. "To be honest, the Broadway version is quite tame; it's quite foursquare, really. We were reinventing it in a style very much *New York, New York*." Since the '82 production, Britten has formed his own opera company, Music Theatre London, whose stagings of *Don Giovanni* and *La Traviata* are on at the Drill Hall while *Guys and Dolls* is in rehearsal. Film music and records, he says, are what have mostly been paying the rent, so that if Sister Sarah is seen to be following the fold, Britten voices the happy feeling that he is 'returning to the fold.'

Run-throughs are unique events insofar as they embody a contradiction. On the one hand, they are clearly unpolished: the odd accoutrement excepted, the actors are not in costume or make-up, and scene changes are done by those seated nearest, whether they be actual stagehands or Eyre, David Toguri, or revival director Fiona Laird, who has been present throughout at rehearsals. Sets, too, are minimal, beyond – in this case – elements of Miss Adelaide's Hot Box and of the sewer scene which the stage management intermittently hammer into (and out of) position.

Conversely, a run-through can deliver an amazing level of performance, since it presents a rare opportunity for the cast to play the show for one another. Once the show is in full production, the logistics of

Henry Goodman hoisted aloft by John Tobias and Anthony Renshaw

Clarke Peters with Joanna Riding in the opening sequence

performance deny them any view of the event as a whole .

'It's the first time they've done it, so everybody fears they'll fall on their face,' says Eyre. 'It's not that you want to show off to your peers, but you want their approval.' Says Henry Goodman: 'Suddenly there's an audience, and there's that sense of urgency about the situations in the piece. Everybody rises up for Richard, for everybody, in order to make it work. There's an enormous amount of adrenalin that carries you through; it's not just chutzpah.'

'We'll do it with the full overture,' says Richard Eyre, and with an excited 'Hit it' to Steven Edis on the piano, the show is off. The hope is to run the musical without interruption, stopping for the interval but otherwise continuing ahead.

The 'Runyonland' overture establishes a New York of long-legged women and largely stooped men, who are more often than not hunched so as to permit the closest possible inspection of the female anatomy. Tom Hodgkins rollerskates through, a Macy's placard around his neck. Street vendors, photographers, policemen – all New York is on view in a cockeyed parade of a gently mythologised Manhattan.

Moments blurred during rehearsal come into focus. Clarke Peters' silken-voice Sky is almost impossibly smooth, a satin guy to Joanna Riding's fiercely determined doll. As their defences drop during 'I've Never Been In Love Before,' opposites attracting in a Broadway moment of magical lyricism, so the reserve of the onlookers melts away. The song finishes and Wayne Cater gets out a handkerchief to blow his nose. (Elsewhere, assistant stage manager Paul Greaves is on hand to feed the odd dropped line.)

Ensnared in what Sky calls 'husband talk,' Henry Goodman's Nathan elevates his henpecked status to the most endearing hilarity. Perhaps it is the actor's own Jewishness coupled with an autobiographical affinity for the material: 'I used to sell watches in Petticoat Lane,' says Goodman , 'so I had a lot of understanding of gambling.' Whatever the reason, he's got not just the accent but the very pith of the part. 'You're always reading books; you're becoming a regular bookie,' he tells Adelaide, demonstrating a winning way with a bad line. Calling later upon Harry the Horse, he lets out a quick whinny.

There have been equally funny Nathans, but few that are as tender. Undoubtedly this Nathan truly loves Adelaide. What Goodman makes clear is that *Guys and Dolls* is the story of a self-confessed 'no goodnick' who is forced, in matters matrimonial, to say yes.

Henry Goodman and Imelda Staunton

He has the ideal partner in Imelda Staunton, and not just because their combined height (or lack thereof) constitutes an unexpected joke all its own next to Peters' lithe, tall Sky. Eliciting wolf whistles during 'Take Back Your Mink,' Staunton stills the room entirely during the reprise of 'Adelaide's Lament.'

In 'Sue Me,' Goodman and Staunton blaze their way through a number whose Yiddishisms ('nu') aren't exactly standard National Theatre fare. They dare, too, to slow parts of the song right down so we see what is at stake: the exasperation and fear that will need to be put aside if Adelaide's visions of domestic bliss are to be realised. Its antics notwithstanding, the duet is larded with deep affection.

And so to 'Sit Down You're Rockin' The Boat' plus two encores – what will happen if more are called for is unclear – with Clarke Peters jivin' by the side of the room as he watches Clive Rowe lead the ensemble in full salvationist exaltation. For all their varying shapes, the cast are swaying as one, and David Toguri leans forward in his chair, locked in concentration.

'Marry the Man Today' – 'you and *me*,' Riding's pert Sarah, ever the grammarian, corrects Adelaide, her newfound cohort in nuptial strategy – leads into the closing scene and a finale that ends in the cast's arms outstretched, as if ready to touch the sky.

'Terrific, really good,' proclaims Eyre, who will wait until the following week to give notes. 'I just cried,' says John Gunter. 'With this cast, the show has really grown; it is going to be a new production, which is wonderful.'

Eyre announces to the company that he will do 'what I'm best at.' And with that, he walks to the side of the room to begin uncorking champagne.

Finale

Imelda Staunton
in the Hot Box

THE END